BLACK WIDOW

The True Story of Giggling Granny Nannie Doss

Ryan Green

Disclaimer

This book is about real people committing real crimes. The story has been constructed by facts but some of the scenes, dialogue and characters have been fictionalised.

Polite Note to the Reader

This book is written in British English except where fidelity to other languages or accents are appropriate. Some words and phrases may differ from US English.

For Helen, Harvey, Frankie and Dougie

CONTENTS

Domestic Goddess

Smooth jazz crackled out of the radio on the kitchen windowsill, and Nannie hummed right along with it. Funny to think that just a few years back that kind of music was the province of rebels and teens, when now you could hear it with the turn of a knob. The late afternoon sunlight was still filtering through the trees outside, and though there was sure to be a chill on the air come morning, Nannie was warm in here beside the open door of her warming oven.

There is a fine art to making pie crust that escapes most home cooks, but Nannie had the knack—hard won through years in the kitchen. She'd cut the shortening with flour and salt until it looked like little peas, then she'd snatch in the jug of water that she'd left cooling out in the shadows on the porch and add it all in one go. Her hands moved on their own, without much need for her intervention, just as her lips pursed and whistled along to the music on the radio.

If her mind had been here, in this moment, then maybe she would have been happy. It was as close to idyllic as any moment of her life so far and much better than most of them. If she could turn her thoughts away from the things that might have been—the things that she longed for so desperately—then maybe she could have settled for this moment as her happiest.

The shock of cold on her fingertips brought her back to the moment at hand with a start. When she looked down, there was a fork in one hand, working away at the crust, and her other hand had gone wandering off across the countertop and brushed against the jug from outside. She giggled at her own silliness, then picked up the little cork-stoppered bottle of vinegar to add just a dash, like mother had taught her.

She should have been happy here, in this kitchen, in this house. Her husband heading home from work to eat his dinner across the table from her. Her days filled with the gentle labours of the completely comfortable. The callouses on her hands from years of hard graft had faded. The aches in her joints on cold mornings were soothed by the warmth of this home that she had made. She should have been happy. Why wasn't she happy?

She fumbled the cork, and vinegar spread across the countertop, filling the whole kitchen with its acrid reek. She snatched up a dishcloth and did her best to mop it up, but she could feel tears pricking at the corners of her eyes. Why wasn't she happy? She had everything that she had ever wanted. She had the husband and the home; she had love in her life. Why wasn't she happy? A sob bubbled up her throat, but she caught it before it escaped and turned it into another giggle. 'Silly me.' No point crying over spilt vinegar, was there? Just another little inconvenience. Hardly worth losing control over. The vinegar hadn't made it far before she righted the bottle and cleaned up. And with a vinegar-soaked cloth, she might as well give the windows a clean when the pie goes into the oven. They didn't need it—sunlight was streaming in—but it was making the best of a bad situation, and that is what Nannie had always been taught to do.

Nannie's hands went back to work on the pie, and she turned inwards again, dreaming of Paris, dreaming of flowers and dancing. Romance had always been her drug of choice, ever since she had been little, and it didn't hurt anybody for her to have a little day-dream. If the man in her dreams didn't look and act exactly like her husband, it wasn't going to hurt anyone. That was the wonderful thing about dreams—you could imagine yourself doing just about anything without ever having to deal with the consequences. You didn't have to think about where you were going to sleep the next day when you'd thrown away your whole life and found yourself cast out into the street. You didn't have to look folk in the eye, knowing that they knew exactly what you had done.

If Nannie could have lived in her dreams, then she would have. What a beautiful life that would be. Breakfast in bed, lunch in some fancy restaurant, carriage rides through the park, bouquets of roses waiting for her behind every closed door, and a single sweet kiss on the lips, just like in the black and white movies that she'd loved ever since the first moment she'd laid eyes on them. True romance. That was what her dreams were made of. There was no sweat dripping in her eyes, there was no grunting or snoring or odious smells, there was just that perfect kiss and then the fade to black.

The fade to black never came. That was the trouble with real life. She had found her husband, he had romanced her, she had melted in his arms and now... nothing. She couldn't just stay melted forever. Life kept on trudging on and wearing her down, and in retrospect, that one perfect moment never quite seemed perfect. She had no shortage of love in her life, but none of it was true. None of it was pure. There was always some ulterior motive, some sordid secret just waiting to be outed. Men were flawed creatures, she understood that—lord, did she understand that—but was it too much to ask for just one of them to truly love her?

She knew love was real, otherwise, how could they have written all those books and songs about it? More than that, though, she knew it was real the same way that she knew there was a sky up above her even when her eyes were closed. Love was a fundamental truth of the universe.

The pie crust was lain out under a clean dishcloth to settle, and her attention was finally turned back to the task at hand. She had a little wicker basket full of apples from the garden, far too sour to eat raw, but sharp and firm, just right for cooking. Her knife danced smoothly through the pale flesh, chopping them into wafer-thin slices that she'd lay across the base and over the top, for texture as much as flavour. A quick dusting of sugar and spice and they were ready.

The prunes were last. Rich and sweet once they were stewed— an old family recipe that her mother and in-laws had all enjoyed, even on their deathbeds. It took more sugar than Nannie would ever admit to get them tasting just right, to be in balance with the apples, but it wasn't like she was going to be eating any of the pie anyway. Her sweet tooth ran in the direction of books and magazines rather than puddings.

Once the prunes were stewing away, Nannie turned her attention to the window panes. She knew that she could be a bit lax when it came to household chores. When her black mood set in it got more and more difficult to find the energy to see to nonsense like scrubbing floors and dusting shelves. Some days it felt like a battle just to get out of bed at all, and her darling husband, the light of her life, would chastise her like she was a spoiled child unwilling to do her share of the chores, even though her share in this house seemed to be every single one of them, while he went slinking off to who knows where with giggling girls half his age. Shameless. He must have thought she was a fool. He must have thought to himself, 'That Nannie is so lost in her daydreams that she won't even notice if I run around on her.'

She had noticed. She noticed everything. She was a dutiful and attentive wife, even when the weight of this miserable life and this horrible little house was pressing down on her like she was pinned in a vice. She knew everything that went on in his life, and he knew not a damned thing about hers, which was exactly the way she liked it.

When he came stomping in, making demands, tossing out her magazines like they were trash instead of treasures, that was when the dark moods came on the strongest. When he left her alone, ran around with teenagers and only slouched in to eat the food that she worked tirelessly to put on his table, it was easier to make believe that everything was going to be okay, that their life together was the true romance of her dreams and not a hollow sham built on a bedrock of lies.

No matter how hard she worked at the windows, she still couldn't see through them clearly. Sunlight should have been streaming right in, but the harder that she tried to see it, the more distant it became. The more that she tried to make it right, the streakier and more opaque the glass became.

Something was burning. The scent of it snapped her out of her furious scrubbing, and she tossed the sour cloth aside into the sink with a grumble. The prunes would be sticking. She stirred at the pot furiously, scraping the wooden spoon across the bottom and hoping that she hadn't wasted a whole tin of prunes on a ruined mess. She stirred and stirred until she was certain that the caramelised fruit was mixed all the way through. She then took a tentative taste. The pie was going to be all right. There was a gristly edge to it that she could taste—a hint that it was burnt and spoiled—but she could pour on more sugar and spice and it would all fade away. Inattention had done that. Something that should have been perfect had almost been spoiled completely just because the one person in the world who was supposed to tend to it had been too busy chasing off after other things. Things that didn't really matter. She could cover it all up, though. She was so very good at covering it all up.

She pulled open the cupboard and let her hands go back to doing things for themselves. Sugar would fix everything. A little more sweetness in their life was exactly what was required. She sprinkled in the white powder and watched with a sigh as it dissolved into the prunes. Just a little more sweetness was all that they needed to make everything come out right.

She set the container of rat poison down beside the sugar packet, then awareness came back to her again, and she giggled at her silliness. She'd forgotten to add the sugar, too. It wouldn't do for that almond flavour to be too bitter. If it was, her husband might not eat enough of the pie. Just one bite wouldn't do. He had to love it so much that he never wanted it to end. He had to guzzle up that pie like it was his last meal on Earth.

Once she was certain of her measurements, Nannie transferred the prunes into the crust and topped it all off with the remaining apple slices and pastry. Once she was satisfied with its perfection, she slipped the pie into the oven and closed the door on it.

Until that moment, the kitchen had remained warm, but now the chill of the evening intruded. That room was the heart of the house, and the heat from her kitchen emanated out to fill the whole space, but with the pie consigned to the oven, there was no longer an excuse to keep on lingering there. Nannie washed off her dishes, threw out the ruined dish-rag and carefully put everything back into its appointed place.

With a sigh, she turned off the radio and headed out into the cold. She wanted the whole house perfect before her husband got home. After all, they'd be getting a mess of visitors soon, and she wouldn't want to shame herself.

Far from Arcadia

Blue Mountain, Alabama, sounds like the kind of place with sweeping fields, scenic vistas, pine forests and hot, humid summers that stretch out long into the latter half of the year, and for the most part that is true. There is some real natural beauty there, but humans have built a legacy of misery right on top of it.

The Hazle farm was far from the idyllic image that most have of rural life. There was more mud than grass and more cursing than praying. James Hazle had inherited it from his parents far younger than he might have expected, and after paying off the loans that they had taken out against future crops that had never even been planted, his inheritance amounted to a few acres of dirt and a few buildings in desperate need of some maintenance. He was alone in the world without a spare penny to hire in help, but, as with so many men, all that he lacked in wealth he made up for in pride. He would have slapped away the hand that offered him charity—not that anyone was ever offering.

His prospects were poor, and the outlook for his future was bleak. No decent woman would marry a man who was certain to lead her into destitution. No bank or seed-loan outfit would front him the cash required to get the farm back in action. He had enough savings and dairy cattle to subsist for a few years, but without a lump sum of money to get things moving his situation was never going to improve.

Lou was in a bad state, too. Try as she might she could not hide her pregnancy from her family any longer, and with no father in the picture, she was destined to be just another one of the many 'ruined women' that Alabama mothers pointed out to their daughters as living warnings about how a sinful life would reward you. Her father took the news about as expected, and if it hadn't been for her mother's rapid intervention he likely would have beaten her until the problem went away. While he was quite content to beat his daughter bloody, he drew the line at hitting his wife. So, with no more recourse to direct violence against Lou for her bad decisions, he switched tactics to the more insidious kind of violence. She was kicked out of the house with no means to support herself—abandoned by her whole extended family until she coughed up the name of the father, so that her father's vicious temper could be turned on him instead and a shotgun wedding could be organised.

Surprising everyone, Lou was resolute in the face of this adversity—whether this was because she genuinely didn't know the identity of the father of her unborn child, or she was so in love with him that she was unwilling to ruin his life the way that he had ruined hers or, most likely, because he was one of the soldiers from the nearby base in Anniston. Whoever fathered her child, she received no financial support from him whatsoever. She scraped by in Blue Mountain by doing odd jobs for a few sympathetic women about town, but the cost of rent on the room that she'd taken was more than she made most weeks.

As she came into the late stages of her pregnancy, Blue Mountain was heading into a fierce winter, and between the cost of wood, the cost of rent, and the minuscule amount of work she was able to do while on the verge of giving birth, Lou ended up in arrears by months with no means to dig herself out of that hole.

Lou's daughter, Nancy, was born out of wedlock on the fourth of November, 1905. She was officially a 'ruined woman' in the eyes of the community, and it was well known by everyone in town that no respectable man would ever have anything to do with her—something that was reported to Lou almost daily by the extended family members who couldn't resist the lure of a cooing new-born baby despite the stigma attached to it.

But Lou just laughed in their faces. No more than a week after the baby had been born, she had received a proposal of marriage from a local farmer. A man with acres to his name, a hardy work ethic, and absolutely no qualms about the fact that Lou had a baby in tow. She was married to James Hazle and settled into her new life on the farm before the end of the year. The town's gossip mill went into overdrive, of course, but it didn't take long before they all settled on the path of least resistance—believing that Nancy Hazle was James' daughter by blood as well as by name and that the timing of events had been the only unfortunate part of their family's story.

If life alone had been hard for Lou, life with James was even harder. She had been starved for even the most basic of human kindness during her pregnancy, and the bare minimum that James had delivered to her then had seemed like a godsend. But now that she was his wife, she was realising with horror that the bare minimum was all that he had to give. James was a dour and miserable man with a mean streak that came out whenever he was put under the least amount of stress.

There was no honeymoon period for Lou. From the moment that she moved into the tiny farmhouse, he started barking orders at her, and when she wasn't pliant or obedient enough for his liking he would lash out with both insults and the cane he used to drive his cattle. Man and wife would be out from dawn working to clear the fields of debris, to plant the crops, to milk the cows. The list of chores that needed doing around the farm was endless, and most nights, they would be up well into the night still trying to get through the tail end of their daily tasks.

Little Nancy, known even then as Nannie, spent most of her early life completely ignored unless she was screaming, an obstacle for the adults to navigate as they went about the back-breaking work of trying to haul the farm back onto its feet. By the time that she was old enough to walk, she was being set to work. As a small child, there was little around the farm that she could physically achieve, but every small and fiddly task that didn't require brute strength was dumped on her, and she received the same harsh punishment as her grown mother if she couldn't work out how to complete her jobs within the allotted time.

James watched her with the slow cogs of his brain turning, calculating how long it would be until she could clear a field of debris, how long until she could be trusted to fetch things from the storehouse or clean the farmhouse by herself so that

Lou could be put to better use. Just as he'd calculate the use of his cattle or any other farm animal, he did the calculations on how long it might be until this little family he had acquired would be yielding the optimal amount of labour, and how much of Lou's labour he was willing to lose if it meant more hands being available further down the line.

One brother and three sisters followed Nannie into the world in rapid succession, all timed carefully so that Lou's pregnancies wouldn't interfere in the harvest.

By the time that Nannie was old enough to retain memories, she knew that she hated her father. As the oldest child, the care of all her brothers and sisters fell to her. She was the one preparing their meals, changing their nappies, and settling their squabbles despite the fact that she was barely more than a child herself. By 1910, when other children her age were heading off to school each morning, Nannie was still trapped at home, taking care of babies and clearing the field of debris ahead of the plough. It was like her life had been put on hold before it even began. Any hopes or dreams that she might have cultivated for the future were ground up and lain as fertiliser for the farm. Despite all of their efforts, the farm rarely did more than break even. Things weren't getting better.

In the winter, when there was less to do around the farm, Nannie and her older brother were permitted to go to school, hiking two miles in the rain and snow to get there, and the same back again. Even that little escape was a miserable experience for her. She couldn't catch up to the other children academically due to the sheer amount of school time she had missed, and even when she did make some gains, they were wiped out in the springtime when she was dragged back to work on the farm all over again. To make matters worse, the other school children looked down on the Hazle kids, correctly identifying them as poor and picking on them for their odd mannerisms and introverted personalities.

Nannie's formal education would never progress beyond her elementary education, even though she was able to attend school more regularly as her brother and sisters got older and started assuming some of her responsibilities. Despite all of this, she developed a lifelong love of reading. In part, this was because the skill had been so hard won for her, and now she was proud of the achievement, but it was mostly because reading was an escape from her unhappy life. With a book, she could be somewhere else, she could be someone else. It was hardly surprising that it posed a tempting alternative to the reality she was trapped in.

Beyond the hateful schoolchildren, Nannie's social life extended only as far as her family tree. When the weather prevented them from carrying on with work at the farm, the whole family would bundle up and head into town to visit with relatives, and when it seemed that the foul weather would persist for more than a few days, they made plans to go even further afield, taking the train out of Anniston to visit family all over Alabama.

In the spring of 1912, as a storm raked the countryside, the Hazle family set out for another visit, this time intending on taking the train down to spend the weekend with some of James' family in the South. The trip started off as well as usual, with all of the dripping wet children slipping and sliding about the carriage until their father barked at them to sit down before they hurt themselves, then moving on to the quieter and more restive phase of the journey when Lou handed out old magazines from her bag, which then settled them. She gave Nannie a battered old copy of True Romance because she knew that it was her favourite, and even though she had read it a dozen times or more, it only took a moment before Nannie was lost in the stories once more. There wasn't much that Lou could do to make her daughter's life better, but the moment that she had discovered Nannie's love for romantic stories, she had started putting aside all the spare change that she could squirrel away to buy more of the yellowing paperbacks and dusty magazines that could sate that hunger.

Nannie was completely lost in the story when everything abruptly went dark. When she next opened her eyes, it was to a world of pain. Her head felt like it was in a vice, and despite it making it worse, she immediately started sobbing. When she managed to force her eyes open, she found that she was laid out on the ottoman in her uncle's house in southern Alabama. The day-long journey had vanished in the blink of an eye. Her mother rushed in when she heard Nannie sobbing and applied a cold compress to her head that nearly knocked her back into unconsciousness with the amount of pain that it inflicted. It would be hours later before that searing pain calmed down enough for Nannie to hear the story of what had happened to her.

The same storm that had freed them from the farm had been whipping across the whole state, and in its furore, it had managed to down a pine tree right by a bend in the railway track. When the driver spotted it, he had slammed on the brakes, flinging everyone onboard forward, out of their seats. The other children had a few bruises and scraped knees, but Nannie had been seated directly in front of a metal bar. When the brakes went on, she had been flung head-first into it and knocked unconscious for the rest of her journey.

At seven years old, Nannie suffered a concussion so bad it left her with permanent damage to her brain. For the rest of her life, she would experience sharp and sudden headaches that could go on for days at a time, and her once bright and cheerful temperament in the face of adversity seemed to have been knocked clean out of her. She was prone to bouts of severe depression from that point on, depression that exhibited itself most often in 'dark moods' that could last even longer than her headaches, but also in brief bouts of uncontrollable rage before she could regain control of herself.

Forbidden Love

A long period of convalescence was not on the cards for Nannie. The moment that they were back on the farm, she was back to work. Over the year that followed, she suffered from blackouts, severe headaches, and long bouts of depression, to the point that seeing her without tears running down her face was considered an oddity. Through it all, James would not allow Lou to take her to a hospital. They had no money to spare, and he couldn't do without the girl around the farm, even if she wasn't quite working at her usual capacity. If she had been an animal, he would have put her down. If she was his daughter by blood instead of marriage, his attitude might have been different, too. It was during this time that the difference in the way that he treated Nannie became the most apparent. He was still hard with the other children, unrelenting in the face of their complaints or failings, but he recognised that they had limits that couldn't be pushed past. With Nannie, and to a lesser extent Lou, he would go on pushing until they were well past the limit of what even he could endure.

Those long months of pain and misery put her treatment at his hands into sharp perspective, and for the very first time in her life, Nannie started to hate. James had made himself the centre of their little world, isolated in the countryside, miles away from their nearest neighbour and denied even the most basic social life thanks to his never-ending demands. He had made it clear that everything that happened in their lives was under his complete control, so when they were miserable and suffering, who else were they going to blame? He had set himself up as the God of Hazle Farm, and that made Nannie, his enemy, the Devil.

With her new black moods and bouts of fury, she was a good fit for that title. It didn't take long before her siblings realised that even though their father had turned away from her, it wasn't safe for them to treat her badly too. Lou was still fiercely protective of her eldest daughter, and while James had set himself above all of them, he was quite happy for his wife to inflict the discipline he felt was so sorely lacking on the children. More pressingly, this new miserable sister of theirs was more than willing to dole out beatings herself when the fury took her, so they took care not to provoke her. She had no fear of the beatings that James would dole out if she was caught hitting her younger brothers and sisters. She was already in constant pain—what was a little more?

It was like Nannie was seeing her father for the first time. He went from being the centre of her world and the focus of all her efforts to a petty bully. He still held an immense amount of power over her, and she was mindful of that, but her devotion to him was broken. The first man that she had ever loved in her life had let her down in the most brutal way imaginable, showing that he didn't care whether she lived or died. It would be a defining moment in her life.

Where before the accident Nannie had enjoyed her mother's romance magazines and books, they now became her obsession. Love became her obsession, the kind that she had read about rather than the coldness she bore witness to between her parents. Her life was going to be like the women's in the magazines. She was going to love and be loved in return, not sink into a routine of misery and hatred that would just go on repeating until somebody died.

Romance became her dream and her sole ambition, to find some lover who would take her away from all of this borderline poverty and back-breaking labour and treat her like the lady she deserved to be. Nothing about life on the farm was romantic. Even the few rural romance stories that Nannie read seemed to be talking about an entirely different place, where every hour wasn't filled with manure, sweat, and berating. Riding bareback on a horse with your hair streaming in the wind sounded like the pinnacle of romance, but that was only if you didn't have to muck out the stalls afterwards.

It is hard to sustain a dream when there is no way to move any closer towards it. There were no dances or town fairs for the Hazle girls. No dating or going out at all if there might be men present. Despite both Nannie and Lou having the seamstress skills to make passably pretty dresses, all of the girls were forbidden from wearing anything that James deemed 'attractive.' He was obsessively possessive of his daughters, and he was convinced that the girls would be molested if he let them roam around wearing pretty clothes or makeup. The one time that he caught Nannie trying to fix up her hair like the girls in the magazines, she received a caning. Even as they headed into their teenage years, none of the girls were allowed to go to town without their father or brother there to serve as a chaperone, and many a long night was spent with them staring wistfully out of the window in the direction of whichever barn was hosting that weekend's hootenanny, straining to hear the sounds of music and dancing.

James was obsessed with maintaining their purity, even though it was something he hadn't valued at all in his own wife. Lou couldn't even argue with him because she knew just how badly sex outside of marriage could go, and he used that shame to bludgeon her whenever she tried to speak up for the girls.

All that Nannie could do was wait and wait for her future to arrive, walking on the knife-edge of desperation between wanting a husband—and the escape that he would bring her from her current state of captivity—and fearing all men as the lecherous animals that her father painted them as.

In the end, the assault did not come from strangers on the outside, as the girls had been trained to expect, but from somewhere closer to home. Even as they grew older, the whole family still continued to travel with James and Lou to visit relatives, including no small number of 'family reunions' that basically devolved into getting drunk in a barn. The extended Hazle family was so sprawling that almost anyone could have attended these events, and while James' vicious outbursts and demand for respect at all costs had been intended to make his girls quiet and pliant, it also made them into the perfect victims for the predators that walked among their relatives. When James discovered an uncle or cousin molesting his daughters, he beat them solidly, and the rest of the family closed ranks against them. It didn't take long before the message spread along every twisted branch of the family tree that they were off-limits. Except for Nannie. When James caught one of his cousins trying to force up her skirt behind the barn when she was only twelve years old, it was she who received the punishment and banishment from the social event. When he caught an uncle unbuttoning her dress, it was she who got sent off to her room for being too flirtatious. The same grapevine for perverts carried the message out to anyone who might want to attend—James didn't give a damn what happened to Nannie Hazle.

James railed against her every time that he got her home after one of those incidents, blaming her for the terrible example that she was setting her younger sisters and making strong implications that the apple hadn't fallen far from the tree, as far as her mother was concerned. This fused Nannie's rage at being molested—when she was meant to be safe—and her hatred of her father, into something new and dangerous. It lit a fire in her and drove her into action, where for years she had been complacent.

Her favourite reading material changed. After years spent on the fantasy of romance, she was now fixated on kicking off her own love story. She set aside the romance magazines and picked up her father's discarded newspapers, locking onto the 'Lonely Hearts' and 'Missed Connections' columns and searching through all of the letters that had been sent in for any that might apply to her. If she could not go to the men, then the men would have to come to her. If she couldn't go on a grand adventure to find the man whom she was meant to be with, then she would have to beckon some brave knight errant to her father's doorstep and expect him to fight for her freedom.

She managed to sneak out a few letters over the months, but if she ever got a response it was intercepted by James before she saw it. He never beat her for attempting to contact men, so presumably they went unanswered.

By 1920, Nannie was fifteen years old, completely done with her faltering attempts at school and ready to move on with her life—another of the many things in life that should have been simple and pleasant that was instead transformed into an arduous battle of wills with James. He did not want to let her out of his sight, particularly now that she was old enough and strong enough to start shouldering all of her mother's burdens around the farm. She knew that an emotional appeal to him would always fall on deaf ears, so instead, she had to come at him with a logically constructed argument in favour of setting her free. James had always been fiercely protective of the accounting work around the farm, even though it was something that Nannie could have been handling (even during her periods of bed-ridden migraines). But still, she had managed to gather from hissed conversations that she heard late at night, and their current state of poverty, that the farm was not making enough money. So, she presented him with a simple solution: let her go out to work. He would lose her labour around the farm, and the amount that she could make in an entry-level factory job wouldn't exceed the amount that she could generate doing her chores, but the money from an external source was regular and guaranteed. It would be a buffer during the long months between crops, and a cushion in case of a cow getting sick or a crop turning out poorly. James slept on it, but come morning, he could think of no decent argument to keep her from doing her part to support the family.

She went out looking for work the very next morning, breathing the sweet summer air, and feeling free for the first time in her life.

First Down the Aisle

It didn't take long for Nannie to secure herself a job at the Linen Thread Mill in Blue Mountain and for her little, brown wage packets to start coming home to brighten up her mother's scowl.

For the first time, it seemed like life on the farm was going to start improving. Nannie's escape from her father's clutches served as an incentive for all of the younger children to start planning for the future, too. Until now, it had seemed that they were all doomed to an eternity working the mostly fruitless fields, but she had shown them that there was a way out. If they could prove that leaving brought more money into the family than their staying, they finally had opportunities and options beyond slowly maturing into clones of their miserable parents. Even still, all of that progress and change was just the first stage in Nannie's grander plan.

Nannie was still barred from wearing makeup by her father, but her clothing choices became less bland as a matter of necessity, so that she could fit in with the rest of the girls at the factory, and as a matter of practicality, since the overblown sack-style dresses that her father preferred would have gotten caught up in the machinery. Allowed to dress like every other girl and out from under her father's looming shadow, Nannie became popular; a social butterfly during working hours. She had friends everywhere that she went in the factory, and since she was in town every day, she ended up as the de facto errand runner for the whole farm too. Before long, it was Nannie whom people in Blue Mountain thought of when they heard the Hazle name, instead of her insular father. She was finally living a normal life, and while others wouldn't have found any joy in it, the novelty still hadn't worn off for her. Everyone she met was greeted with a smile; every little bit of help that she could give to others, she gave.

She was the pride of Blue Mountain, and that popularity was not limited to the other women. Older men were cautious in their approach to her—she was still very young, for all that she was pretty, and nobody wanted the reputation of chasing after children. She received no small amount of admiration from the single men about town, but it was always restrained, even though she clearly relished every compliment.

As a prospect for marriage for most of the farming community, she was a shaky proposition, although not nearly as risky as her mother had been. Most women would still have been expected to bring a dowry or the promise of some property along with them when they married, but it was widely known that the Hazle farm was both too small to be portioned up and too poor to provide much in the way of financial incentive. Taking a pretty young thing like Nannie for a bride was considered to be an extravagant luxury that only the wealthy could indulge. Romantic ideas were all well and good, but survival was still the primary concern of most people in rural America, even as late as the 1920s.

Luckily, the old men of Blue Mountain were far from being Nannie's only prospects. The factory itself was packed to bursting with eligible young men, and while their parents may still have had enough influence to steer the majority of them away from the charming young Nannie, some of them were either too stubborn to be steered or lacking in parental guidance.

Nannie took up smoking so as to have an excuse to linger outside the factory with all of the boys, and she was making good enough money at the factory that even her father never bothered to complain about the frivolity of her minor habit. But despite making herself available out in the yard, it was actually in the noisy factory itself that most of them approached her. Out in the yard she held court, but when it came time for the actual advances to be made, the young men wanted the relative privacy that the machine noise could provide.

With her mother's example firmly in mind, Nannie made it clear to all of her suitors that she was only interested in marriage and not a dalliance. That was enough to put off most of the teenagers who had been pursuing her, but certainly not all. One boy in particular, Charley Braggs, was so smitten with her that he almost proposed on the spot.

Charley was seventeen years old, tall and handsome with a head of curly hair and a smile that even managed to melt the heart of the extremely dubious Lou Hazle on the single evening that he was invited home to the farm for dinner. Of all Nannie's potential suitors, he was the only one who managed to win over both Lou and James—Lou with his charm and good looks and James with his uncommon nature. While other boys his age were hanging out in the cafés and gin mills of Anniston, listening to jazz music and cavorting, Charley had a more solitary nature, spending his paycheques on the careful upkeep of his family home and on the care of his sickly mother. Respect for your elders was a constant theme in James' preaching to his children, so it was hardly surprising that this devotion won young Charley some points with the old man.

James clearly didn't care much about the gossip about town and did no prying into the boy's history or family. If he had been worried about those things then he would never have married Lou to begin with, and as far as Nannie was concerned, he felt that beggars could not be choosers. If this boy was willing to take the cost of caring for the rebellious Nannie off his hands permanently, then he was happy for him to do so as soon as possible.

Just four, short months after they began courting, Nannie and Charley walked down the aisle together. She brought nothing with her but a drawer full of home-made clothes and the promise that she would try her best to be a good wife to him.

This was hardly the grand romance that she had always dreamed about. There were no flowers or fancy meals, she wasn't whisked away to an exotic locale or showered with gifts. It barely even contained the level of romance that you might have expected from a usual teenage courtship. Charley spent a little bit of time with her, but with neither of them allowed a social life outside of work hours, that left only the few family meals that he attended in the intervening months, which hardly lent themselves to grand romantic gestures.

From her sporadic diary entries in 1921, we can see that Nannie felt that she was forced into the marriage. She felt as if the great escape that she had been orchestrating had just been undercut entirely by James' compliance and, indeed, delight at the prospect of her marriage. While she had still been testing the waters with other suitors, Charley had pressed his proposal on her through her father, and as a group, the family had railroaded her into it. Instead of being the most wonderful moment in her life, the wedding felt like a transaction taking place, the way that her father would buy or sell a cow.

The ceremony was uninspiring and sparsely attended on Charley's side. His mother was there, and a trio of the guys from work, but he didn't have many friends. His complete absence of a social life didn't leave much time for maintaining relationships, and the majority of the guys at work who were about his age were sore because he'd swooped in on Nannie. Nannie's side of the church was a lot fuller, with her extended family descending like vultures at the first sign that there might be a free meal and some liquor. While she was on good terms with all of the girls at work, she had never developed any particular friends, so her blanket invite had only drawn out a few of the older factory women, who were mostly there to say goodbye to her as they didn't expect she would still be working much after the wedding. They were completely right, of course, she had no intention of working again. That wasn't part of her grand plan.

Despite the specifics of the husband being slightly different from what she might have intended, Nannie planned to be the perfect wife. She would keep the house, raise the babies, cook all of the meals, and excel any expectations that Charley might have had for her. Her love and support would help him to flourish, and out from the controlling whims of her father she might finally find a little bit of enjoyment in her own life. This was her chance to finally break free of controlling parental figures and start living her life, and while he might not have been her first choice, at least she was confident that the quiet and undemanding Charley would be easy enough to manipulate into doing what she wanted, a scenario which was the complete opposite of her obstinate and abusive father.

Mother Knows Best

After the ceremony and the party were over, Nannie was brimming with excitement. She lived on a farm, so she was well aware of the mechanics of sex, and at a young age, she had made the connection between the physical act and the 'marital bliss' that she had read about so widely. Sex was the undercurrent of every romantic story that she had ever read, even if it was forbidden for them to even write about it. It had also served as the primal backdrop for her own life story, too, serving as the motivation behind the amorous overtures of all the young men she had met, the horror story of her mother's extra-marital pregnancy, the drive behind her molestation at the hands of relatives, and now her marriage, where she was allowed, finally, to enjoy this secret pleasure that she had so long been denied.

In the early evening, they arrived at Nannie's new home, the first place that she would ever truly be able to call hers. They would deal with the petty details of squaring away gifts and putting away her little suitcase of clothes in the morning. The young lovers only had eyes for each other. From all accounts, Charley had a perfectly pleasant evening, but for Nannie, the crushing anticlimax of her first intimacy wasn't the perfect end to the day that she'd had. Still, she reasoned that things might get better and less painful with time. Her own mother had intimated as much during the extremely vague talk that she had given to Nannie about 'wifely duties' at the party. Things were not perfect, as she had always dreamt they would be, but they were not ruined, either.

She still had hope for her future, until she came down the stairs in the morning and found her mother-in-law seated at the kitchen table, glowering at her with a contemptuous sneer on her face. 'Charley will be needing his breakfast before work. Best I go wake him while you see to it.'

Nannie had barely met Mother Braggs before the wedding, in no small part because of the woman's ill health, which had flared up every time a social engagement involving the Hazle family was scheduled. She looked remarkably healthy now as she barked out orders, but Nannie did her best to calm her foul temper. After all, this situation was only temporary; she was surprised that his mother seemed to have stayed over in their house last night without anyone telling her, but at least she wouldn't have to endure the woman's sharp tongue for long.

When Charley came down, he walked right past the plate she had prepared for him to kiss his mother on the cheek before saying 'good morning,' and it took almost the entire time that he was getting ready for work before Nannie managed to corner him and politely ask when his mother would be heading home.

'She is home, silly. She lives here with us.'

Nannie was so stunned that she didn't even have a chance to form any sort of counter-argument before he was out the door and heading off to work. She spent the rest of the day performing household chores under the watchful eye of her new mother-in-law, and while the woman wasn't likely to beat her as James used to, she found fault in absolutely everything that Nannie did. Nothing was up to the standards that she expected in her home, and she expected Nannie to repeat every task until she got it right. In the end, Nannie barely made it through a quarter of the jobs that she had intended to attend to on her first day, and she was exhausted and miserable by the time that Charley came back to take it all in with dismay.

She had traded one slave master for another, and while she felt no qualms about defying her own father, each time she said anything even the slightest bit critical about her new mother-in-law it seemed to physically wound Charley.

She was trapped in a web of social obligation and politeness, more surely than the threats of violence had ever held her. In front of her son, Mother Braggs was nothing but magnanimous with Nannie, barely even correcting her when mistakes were made around the house. Barely speaking loud enough for Charley to hear the litany of his new wife's many faults. Charley's mother had spent a lifetime alternately spoiling and manipulating her son, and she had it down to a fine art.

Mother Bragg was a single parent in much the same way that Nannie's mother had been, but while Lou had been saved from a lifetime of shame and disaster at the last moment, the same could not be said for her counterpart. Charley had been raised in abject poverty until an early inheritance lifted them onto the property ladder, and from an early age, he was groomed to be the man of the house and provider for his mother. What had started as flattery about his maturity had soon been transformed into truth as he was sent out to work, and no small part of his personality had been carefully moulded by his mother to ensure that he would always put her wants and needs first.

Nannie had expected to be able to work her way around Mother Braggs when Charley was home, and she couldn't risk showing her true colours in front of her son, but the older woman had too much experience to be so easily thwarted. If Nannie wanted to go out for a meal with her husband, Mother Braggs would be suffering from a stomach complaint. If she wanted to go to the pictures, Mother would have a dizzy spell and they'd end up sitting around the kitchen table playing Mah-jong yet again. The social life that Nannie had been so desperately craving was held just out of reach once more, and her daily life was just getting more and more miserable.

The fantasy world of romance had been stolen from her by the constant demands on her time. Even though her own chance at a 'happily ever after' had been stripped away from her, she had hoped to at least find some escape in her beloved stories, but Mother Braggs viewed the reading of romances as akin to infidelity and destroyed, on sight, any magazines that Nannie managed to smuggle into the house. For a while, they played cat and mouse, with Nannie seeking out hiding places for her reading materials and the old woman hunting for them, but eventually it came to a head when Mother Braggs laid out in excessive detail, in front of Charley, how pleased that she was to see Nannie wasn't filling her head with such childish nonsense like other, more frivolous girls her age. With the two of them now on the lookout, she abandoned all hope, beyond browsing the racks at the local store.

One by one, her avenues of escape were closed off. Nannie's relationship with her own mother had always been good, even though she viewed Lou as powerless to stop the worst excesses of James' behaviour. She was still an ally against him, though, and she had still been the closest thing to a friend and confidant that Nannie had ever had. Even in married life, she had expected to still see Lou regularly and even intended on baking up fancy afternoon teas for when she came to visit. When Lou did come, she received a frosty reception from Mother Braggs and was always put out of the house immediately after supper, with any suggestion that she might stay the night being immediately torn apart. For his part, Charley seemed to be almost entirely oblivious to the whole situation, as much as he was to everything else going on in his home. Whatever his mother said was the law as far as he was concerned, with there being no point in arguing about it.

With desperation mounting, Nannie started looking for alternate avenues of escape. The smoking habit that she had used as an excuse to step out of work became a ward against Mother Braggs—who detested the smell but couldn't find a way to demand that Nannie quit without sounding unreasonable—and then it became an addiction, with the newlywed puffing her way through forty or more cigarettes a day. Worse still, she turned to the Braggs' liquor cabinet for some relief from the grinding disapproval and disappointment.

Alcohol may have eased the pain briefly, but it didn't take long before messing around with her brain chemistry came back to bite Nannie. The entirely reasonable bouts of depression she was experiencing after seeing her dream snatched away were now accompanied by a constant smog. Her dark moods went from being a rare visitor to a constant companion. There was not a single day that she didn't feel like just curling up in a ball and dying rather than going through the motions of trying to please Mother Braggs all over again. In a strange way, it was actually that antagonistic relationship that saved Nannie's life. She couldn't just lie in bed all day, because that would prove all of Mother's insinuations about her laziness correct. She couldn't just lie down and die, because that would mean letting the old hag win.

The old defiance that had characterised Nannie's relationship with her father came back to the fore, and she powered through each day ignoring every word that Mother had to say and pretending that the old woman wasn't spending every waking moment whispering about her failings into Charley's ear.

After three years of labouring to please her mother-in-law, Nannie put the old woman out of mind, because, ultimately, she had two vital—but related—weapons in her arsenal that Mother Braggs could never hope to match. For the first three years of their marriage, she gave Charley all the sex that he wanted, whenever he wanted it. And when his interest in the carnal began to fade, along with her novelty, she gave him children, binding him to her forever, despite the loathing that she had grown to feel for the spineless runt she had been bullied into marrying.

They had four daughters, one a year between 1923 and 1927, with the eldest named Melvina and the youngest named Florine. In-between her pregnancies, Nannie came to loathe the touch of Charley. He was still as gormless as ever, completely unaware of her suffering or even the exhaustion that motherhood had brought along with it. She suffered through sex with him only rarely and only when the timing was right to ensure she would become pregnant again. Otherwise, she avoided their marital bed as much as possible, taking to sleeping in the children's room in case they needed her in the night and to her finding comfort elsewhere.

With children in the picture, there was no longer much of a threat that Mother Braggs could do anything to terminate the marriage, and so Nannie's contempt for her grew. All of the complaints and snipes that wounded Nannie in the early days of her marriage now fell on deaf ears, and if Mother went telling tales to Charley, then he never acted on the information.

When either Lou or Mother Braggs could be pressed into service as a babysitter, Nannie would leave her children and head out to the gin mills of Anniston to find men who could make her feel beautiful again, the way she felt when the whole world was courting her. Stories filtered back to Lou about her daughter's harlotry, about the girl roaming bars topless, being fondled in public and going off into back rooms with drunkards. Nannie was trying to wash away all of the pain in a sea of gin and sex, but it was never enough, and in the morning the hangover and black moods would sweep back in, along with the shame.

Neither Charley nor his mother could ever confirm any of the stories that were being told about Nannie's infidelity, and Charley was living in a glass house as far as that was concerned, having struck up several brief but lacklustre affairs with young women in the Linen Thread Mill over the years. Nannie knew all about them and kept notes on them in her diaries so that she could use them against Charley if he ever tried to go against her or end their marriage unfavourably.

When it came to her daughters, Melvina was the apple of Nannie's eye, the girl into whom she poured all of her own hopes and dreams. Melvina was going to go on to live a wonderful life. She was going to have a grand romance and never have to settle for a lesser man. Everything that Nannie had once imagined for herself she promised to Melvina.

Her own life had gone appallingly off track, and every child after Melvina became an even greater burden for her to bear. Suddenly, she wasn't just cooking, cleaning, dressing, and coddling for her husband and his mother, but also for four children under the age of five. Her every waking moment was punctuated by the screams and demands of one of the six, and those brief moments of respite that she had bought herself with liquor, smoking, and escape into the arms of other men became fewer and fewer.

Meanwhile, Charley's own infidelities were becoming more and more obvious to everyone around him. While Nannie had mastered the art of putting on a smile and pretending that everything in her life was perfect around Blue Mountain, he had made his unhappiness abundantly clear to anyone who would listen, and if he ever found a woman with a sympathetic shoulder for him to cry on, it didn't take him long to turn the relationship sexual. He would often disappear for two or three days at a time with his new paramours, abandoning Nannie to deal with everything by herself and providing barely any more support than that, even when he was physically present. It got to the point that the two of them only met by accident—at the dinner table or in the bedroom. They were both alone in the relationship, but while Mother Braggs, along with the many women that he bedded, was there to give Charley an emotional outlet, there was no such comfort for Nannie. Just like in her childhood, she was completely isolated from the community, at large by the controlling parental figure in her life, and for all that she still dreamed of a great romance, nobody was fool enough to actively court her while she was married. She probably would have looked on anyone that tried to do such a thing as despicable.

So, the days rolled on and on, grinding her down a little more with each passing moment. Hangovers and depression clouded her mind and dogged her every step. Unless something drastic happened, Nannie felt certain that she was going to be ground away to nothing.

The Practicalities

Nannie's overwhelming love for her children was apparent to everyone—in the eyes of Mother Braggs it was the girl's only redeeming feature—but they went very rapidly from being the centre of her world because she was so smitten with them, to being the centre of her world because they were so demanding of her attention at all times. She would often go days without sleep because one child or another had an illness, or simply because they weren't tired because their grandmother had decided to put them down for a nap in the middle of the day when she was watching them and Nannie was out running errands.

Even when she was in her darkest moods, Nannie was able to fake a smile for her daughters, but gradually, every single smile that she mustered for them was fake. Whatever joy she had found in becoming a mother was over, and the reality of being a mother for the rest of her life sank in. She tried to keep on going, focusing only on the practicalities, even when she found her love for her children faltering, but as she grew more and more desperate, the practical solution to the problem became more and more apparent. She had too many children to care for.

At almost five years old, Melvina registered in Nannie's mind as another human being and as somebody that she felt she had a strong emotional tie to, even though that connection was currently numbed by her circumstances. The other three were the problem. She could still remember what it felt like to have only one child to care for, back when her husband was still at least partially present and the security that Melvina provided had given her the courage to stand up to her overbearing mother-in-law. There had been no point in her life where she felt as contented or as capable as in that first year of motherhood. She could be an amazing mother when she only had one child to care for, when she could focus her attention entirely on one child's needs and still have enough time left to care for herself.

It was a simple equation in Nannie's mind. She could have four miserable children and live her own life in a constant haze of depression and exhaustion, or she could have one happy and healthy child who would go on to do amazing things with her life. It was no choice at all.

The next time that Charley returned from one of his three-day benders, the whole town of Blue Mountain seemed to be camped out in his house. He had to push through the crowd to get inside, and as hungover and bewildered as he was, he accepted all of the hugs and condolences without any understanding of what had happened at all. When all of the black clothes started to sink into his brain, he immediately panicked, thinking that his mother had died. But before long, he located her in the kitchen, holding court with the other women of a certain age. Charley pushed his way back through to the sitting room, where he finally spotted Nannie at the centre of it all. Her mother was sitting by her side, her father lurking by the window, very deliberately making no comment on where the hell his son-in-law had been. The baby was pressed to her side, snoozing gently, and Melvina sat by her feet, with Nannie gently stroking her hair. The other two were conspicuous in their absence. 'Where are the girls?'

Whispers and mutters started spreading through the crowd as people slowly realised that Charley still didn't know. Morbid curiosity turned all eyes his way. He could feel the weight of their scrutiny, a whole town wondering where he had been, what he had been doing, why he hadn't been here for his family when they needed him the most. Nannie let the tears flow and was enveloped in the comforting arms of her mother and every other woman nearby, and James took Charley firmly by the arm and dragged him away so that nobody could see the boy break.

Florine was still breastfed, and Melvina had eaten nothing but toast on that fateful morning, so whatever had gone wrong with the porridge grain passed her over. But the middle two had eaten their breakfast and went off giggling with the same reckless abandon as had often plagued Nannie's days. By lunchtime, neither one of them could even walk. The doctor had been rushed out and recognised the signs of acute food poisoning, but medical science had no answer to it. If it had been caught immediately then vomiting could have been induced before the sickness set in, but nobody had suspected anything was awry. Even Mother Braggs, usually ready to condemn Nannie in an instant for the tiniest mistake, could find no fault in her actions. Their daughters were dead, and

Charley hadn't even been there to say goodbye. For the first time in his life, Charley felt the weight of his mother's disapproval, amplified a thousandfold by the scrutiny of the town.

In the midst of this circus, Nannie sat with huge, unshed tears hanging in her dark eyes, staring out at Charley, her eyes pinned to him everywhere that he went. She didn't say a single word to him. She didn't damn him for his absence nor confide in him about her grief. She didn't seem to care about him one way or the other. Over the coming days, she seemed to silently revel in all of the attention and sympathy that she was receiving, and the girls' death was, at large, treated by the town like some terrible act of God, one that Nannie was deemed as heroic for enduring with such stoicism. Everywhere that Charley went, people were singing Nannie's praises, and even in his own home, in the company of his own mother, his attempts to complain about her were cut off short. 'You'll never understand how a woman loves her babies, so don't you say a word against your wife until all this is settled and done.'

The funeral came almost immediately, with Nannie feigning desperation to get it all over with and the townsfolk more than willing to oblige. There was no delay from the state's side, either—the doctor had observed the children in their last moments and diagnosed the problem on the spot. There was no need for an autopsy—only to throw away the tainted grains that had killed them. There wasn't even a hint that Nannie could have done anything wrong since her house was known to always be spotless and her cooking the envy of husbands everywhere. Despite everything that happened, she still managed to prepare a beautiful spread of food for after the funeral too.

Whispers had dogged Charley's footsteps ever since he came back to find his life in ruins. He had gone from being a liked man to the subject of scorn and contempt. As Nannie's star rose, so his fell. By the time of the funeral, he actually began to seriously consider the possibility that he had done wrong by his wife and family, that he was the source of the unhappiness that had plagued their home since the very beginning. After all, everyone could see how perfect Nannie was. All except him. Even her most stalwart detractor, Mother Braggs, was treating Nannie like a precious angel. But all of that self-loathing and doubt came to an abrupt end when Nannie laid a plate of food down in front of him and gave him a well-practised, sad smile. He hadn't been able to look her in the eye since he'd gotten back into town—shame and dread that she might give him sympathy and crumble his broken heart to pieces had kept him from wanting to—but now he met her dark eyes and was paralyzed with fear. There was nothing in them. She wasn't sad. She wasn't angry. All of the human emotions that you might have expected to find were just absent, and in their place was a dark and fathomless void. One that he had helped to create.

In the dead of night, with two of his children fresh in the ground, Charley packed his bags, grabbed Melvina from her bed and ran for his life. He had no doubt in his mind that Nannie had killed their daughters and even less doubt that now she had a taste for the town's sympathy and adoration she would soon seek to make herself into a widow as well. Florine was nestled in Nannie's arms when Charley made his escape or he would have taken her away too.

The outpouring of sympathy for Nannie redoubled when her husband's treachery was discovered. To begin with, she had tried to treat it as just another one of his binges, but the fact that he had stolen away in the night with Melvina told her that she wasn't so lucky. For a while, she got to live the life that she had wanted, socialising with the people around town, living more or less alone and unbothered in the Braggs' house with only the hint of her mother-in-law still haunting it, but any enjoyment she might have taken in having her wishes fulfilled was tarnished by the loss of Melvina. If she could have rid herself of Florine without suspicion, she probably would have done so, but Melvina had been everything to her.

1927 was the longest year of Nannie's life as she drifted along aimlessly, refusing every offer from her mother to come home and bring the baby with her. The meagre savings of the Braggs family soon dwindled, and she was forced to take up work in a cotton mill to support not only herself and her daughter but her malingering mother-in-law too. At least that last mouth to feed demanded only very little. Mother Braggs had been shocked by her son's actions and begun to decline not long after. Her 'ill health,' which had only previously flared up when she was trying to manipulate her son, had now become a constant and all-too-real presence in her life. She was racked with stomach pains so severe that most days she couldn't get out of bed and was forced to rely on the kindness of Nannie for her survival. Despite all that had happened, Nannie still fed and watered the old woman every day, going so far as to stew prunes for her each day to try and ease her aching guts. It was all for nothing in the end—Mother Braggs expired in the Summer of 1927, with her son still missing and absolutely no doubt on the part of the townsfolk that her death was due to natural causes. After all, she had spent so many years plagued by this illness, it was hardly surprising that it had finally taken her.

Nannie had the whole house to herself, although she could hardly afford a fraction of its upkeep, and legally, Charley remained the sole owner. It was a curious state of limbo, where she had everything that she wanted and nothing at the same time, unable to move on with her life until her errant husband finally re-appeared to release her but dreading it all the same.

As the leaves began to turn and the balmy summer faded into a mild winter, Nannie fought to find her equilibrium. Working full-time and caring for her baby the rest of the time was still a huge relief compared to the workload that she had once faced, but even with only two mouths to feed she found that she struggled without his income, and the house began to slip into disrepair. More importantly, she was intensely lonely once more. Back at home, she had her mother and siblings to distract her from the void in her life where socialising would usually have gone, but no matter how charming and pleasant she was, she lacked the fundamental skills required to form friendships any deeper than the casual acquaintances she'd enjoyed at the Linen Thread Company. Her father had seen to that by isolating her through her formative years. The only relationship that she had ever had that had any substance, was with Melvina, and she had been stolen from her in the night.

In the summer of 1928, Charley came home, arriving unannounced in a taxi from Anniston with Melvina, a strange woman, and a little boy. Nannie stood in the doorway of the house and watched them approaching, fury building in her chest.

Charley had never had trouble attracting members of the opposite sex, and while having a daughter in tow put a slight cramp on his style, it didn't take him long to start using her to his advantage. Realising that he didn't know the first thing about cooking, cleaning, or raising a child himself, he set out to find himself a replacement mother, and before a month was out he had settled into a comfortable enough life with a widow, who had a son about Melvina's age, a few towns over. In theory, his life was just as comfortable as before—even better when you took into account his much more agreeable 'wife'—but something still felt wrong to Charley. He felt like he had been run out of town instead of choosing to leave willingly, and if he was being honest with himself, he had run not because of the judgement of the town but because he was genuinely afraid of Nannie.

There was no logical way to explain it. With her soft curls and rounded face, Nannie looked almost cherubic, and she was so obviously good-natured that her kindness and devotion to her family were the talk of the town. The longer that Charley was away from her, the more that he remembered all of this and wondered what on earth he had been so afraid of. Nannie was a soft, sheltered farm girl. Every time that he paid rent on his new place, he felt resentment bubbling up. Why should he be paying rent while Nannie was living in the lap of luxury in his own home for nothing? When news of his mother's death finally filtered through, and he knew that he would no longer have to face the weight of her disapproval on top of his fears, he became resolute to return home and drive Nannie out.

She stood in the doorway looking just how he remembered her: perfect and pristine with his daughter nestled on her hip. For just one moment he turned back the clock and saw her the way he had first seen her, holding court in the factory yard, men hanging on her every word, rushing to light her cigarette. A hint of glamour amongst the dirt of daily life. A smile tickled at his lips, then he forced it away, chasing off any joy he might have taken in his marriage in the cavalcade of complaints against Nannie, both his mother's and the ones that he had manufactured to reflect them. After all, his mother was always right, and he felt certain that she would have approved of his new girlfriend much more. She was much more respectable, apart from her willingness to shack up with a married man.

They exchanged very few words. Nannie knew that this day would come. She had no illusions that Charley was going to come rushing back and sweep her up in his arms like she had always dreamed. Anything resembling a romantic dream about him had long since withered away in the face of the sad reality that he was just a spoiled, stupid, little boy.

She packed up her clothes, and the children's, took Melvina from his unresisting arms, and walked away from them both. She stole whatever triumph he might have felt at driving her out from under him and left with dignity, despite the fact that the darkest and most murderous mood she had ever experienced in her life had just descended upon her. Nannie's face was arranged into a mask of sadness as she walked by the new Braggs family, and Charley's new wife was overwhelmed with sympathy for her despite all of the horror stories that she had been told. But Charley himself caught another glimpse of the darkness behind Nannie's eyes, and he felt that same bone-chilling terror that had driven him away from home the first time. If he had been alone, he had little doubt that she would have killed him at the first opportunity. Time would prove this assumption to be correct.

Hope Springs Eternal

Nannie returned to the family farm and the constant demands of her father. Lou was delighted to have the grandkids under her roof, but James expected Nannie to immediately resume her duties around the place now that her marriage had failed. The farm was still doing poorly and would continue to do poorly in perpetuity. The divorce papers came through promptly, and Nannie was happy to sign away her marriage so long as the reason listed for the divorce was Charley's infidelity. Given that he was currently living with another woman and a child that referred to him as 'Daddy,' it wasn't exactly hard to swing that addendum. After eight years, her first marriage was dissolved.

With Melvina home at last, Nannie promptly forgot about her obsession with her daughter. She still liked Melvina, loved her even, but the all-consuming fixation on her daughter faded away to nothing in the face of actually having a relationship with the six-year-old. It may have been the most important relationship in Nannie's life, but that didn't mean that it was even slightly fulfilling.

Rather than endure the day-long nagging of her father and, increasingly, her mother, Nannie sought work to get her out of the house and away from them all. Charley had resumed his old entry-level position in the thread mill in Blue Mountain where they had first met, so that avenue was closed off to her. The other mill where she had found work had employed her only as a seasonal worker and dropped her as soon as her divorce became public knowledge, so that offered no recourse either. With no other option, she began looking further afield and finally settled into a job in a cotton mill over in Anniston. The commute was a nuisance, the work was hard, and the conditions in the mill were so hot as to be just barely tolerable. But in addition to paying better than any work she had ever done in Blue Mountain, it also provided her with long periods away from the farm and all of the male attention that she could have asked for.

Four pregnancies and a divorce had done nothing to temper Nannie's natural beauty, and she spent almost every moment at work being admired by the many men that staffed the machinery. She relished this attention, and it did a lot to assuage her wounded ego to have so many men lusting after her, but that did not mean she was ready to jump into bed with one of them again so quickly. She was never going to make the same mistake again, marrying a man just because he was the first to offer, and she would ensure that her parents had no say in any of her future romantic arrangements, just to be on the safe side.

She carefully vetted every one of her suitors at the Anniston mill and found every single one of them wanting. The young ones were still too much in the sway of their parents, and there was nothing that Nannie dreaded more than the idea of inheriting another slave-master along with whatever man she settled for. As for the older ones, men who had worked in the mill all their lives were either sorely lacking in ambition or too badly injured by the mill work to fit in anywhere else. It wasn't that they repulsed Nannie, it was just that there was no possibility of them fulfilling her romantic fantasies, so she immediately discounted them. She was done with settling for anything less than true love, even if that meant that it took her a little longer to find it.

Loneliness had always been the cornerstone of Nannie's psyche. Her long, isolated childhood followed by her loveless marriage had compounded that feeling into a drive that would persist through the rest of her life. The romance magazines that she hoarded and reread over and over helped to ease the ache for a while, but that couldn't last. She needed to find somebody to fill that void, to make her whole. And so she turned from one of the great comforts of her childhood to the other: the 'Lonely Hearts' columns.

Looking back on the letters she had sent out as a desperate teenager, the now adult Nannie found them equally endearing and naive. Now that she had experienced a sexual relationship, she could recognise the undertones littering the listings. Some of the men she had replied to before had been looking for something very different from what she had offered up, so it was hardly surprising that none of her first batch of replies had gotten a response. With maturity and experience, Nannie was now able to add a whole new layer to her fantasies and reflect those fantasies back to the men that she was in communication with.

She had a photograph taken to send out along with the letters and baked goods that she began to distribute, but it didn't do her any justice. Without the sparkle of life in her eyes and the tiny hint of a smile that came and went from the corner of her mouth, she looked almost average, instead of being instantly recognisable as a woman of distinction. But whatever was lacking in the visual stimulation that she sent along was more than compensated for in other ways. Her baking had always been the pride of the Hazle family, and even Mother Braggs had never been able to find fault in it. So, too, were the few men that she graced with a reply ensnared by her pies. And if the taste of home cooking wasn't enough to win the men over, the letters that she sent out along with those pastries were right on the verge of being lewd.

For several months, this was Nannie's whole life—fastidiously replying to every letter that she received, combing through the newspaper for new contenders for her heart, and feeling for the first time like it was possible that her dream of romance might come to pass. In person, men were always fairly naked in their desires for her, but by letter, they were forced to dress their sordid desires with poetry and prose to win her over. It was like being in one of her romance novels—she was finally being spoken to like she was the star of her own story rather than an afterthought or impediment.

Out of all the many suitors that she considered, there was only one that went beyond an exchanging of letters. In 1929, Nannie received a letter of beautiful verse and a photograph of a man who could have been a film star, with the wavy hair of Grant Withers and the dimpled chin of Clark Gable. Robert Franklin Harrelson, known to one and all as Frank, was a twenty-two-year-old factory worker from nearby Jacksonville.

Two years Nannie's junior, he nonetheless impressed his maturity upon her—especially when compared to her ex-husband. He lived alone in a modest apartment in the city, where he had acquired an average social life and a love of jazz music. In reply to his charming letter, Nannie replied with a slice of spice cake, a copy of her photograph, and a letter of her own that was less poetic but carried a powerful subtext.

The day after her reply was sent, there was a knock on the door of Hazle farm. Frank had finished reading her letter and immediately jumped in the car to drive down to see this beauty in person. He was stunned when the real Nannie answered the door. In person, she was vibrant and charming, in a way that no letter or picture could convey. He was utterly smitten with her, and more than ready to just load her into the car and take her home with him on the day. Over the next few weeks he would visit her frequently, showering her with the kind of romantic gifts that she had always dreamed of but learned not to hope for. Flowers, chocolates, lace, and more arrived in carefully wrapped packages with more of Frank's charming poetry attached. A gentleman like that was enough to turn any girl's head, but for Nannie, with her dreams of a grand romance, it was intoxicating beyond anything she had ever experienced before.

He proposed to her only two months after they'd met for the first time, and she accepted without a second thought. He was a dream made flesh, a larger than life character from out of one of the talkies—how foolish would she have had to be to play coquettish now that her new life was in sight.

Frank had grander dreams than any of the men that she'd dallied with before. He planned to take her away from all of this, to start a new life without the interference of her family or the judging gaze of the people of Blue Mountain. Before the wedding was even planned, he had secured a new job for himself at the Goodyear Textile Mill in Cedartown, Georgia— no great step up from his current role in a Jacksonville factory, but with better prospects for advancement and the added allure of a more exotic locale.

Nannie's second wedding was attended by more people than could fit in the church, with the whole town of Blue Mountain turning out to wish her well and see her off to her new life— one last sign of solidarity with a woman who had suffered so much, so young. The only ones who seemed unhappy with the arrangement were Nannie's parents. They had not been consulted on the marriage in the least, and while Lou had been easily won over by Nannie's doe eyes and fluttering heart, her father was less inclined to take her feelings into account, preferring to judge Frank by his own merits, which he judged to be lacking. No man who was worth a damn would have to use such pretty words to get around folks, after all.

The one point that both of Nannie's parents were in agreement upon was the grandchildren. Since returning home, Melvina and Florine had basically been adopted by Lou, while Nannie was off working all hours and writing letters the rest. And now, without warning, they were going to be ripped from her arms and hauled off across the country where they might never see them again. Of course, all that Nannie had to do to silence any complaints from either one of them was to invoke the name of Charley Braggs.

Despite Lou and James' complaints, Nannie, Frank, and the girls all loaded into the car with suitcases crammed full of all their worldly belongings and set off northeast without a backwards glance towards their new home. Frank had just enough in savings to put down a deposit on a two-bedroom log cabin just outside of Cedartown, a meagre enough place compared to some of the homes Nannie had lived in, but a perfect fulfilment of so many fantasies that romance stories had instilled in her.

With the kids safely stowed away in their bedroom and the night drawing in, the two of them made love by the log fire. It was perfect. This was the end of the story that she had been weaving in her mind throughout her life, when everything would be settled and she would live happily ever after.

But the fade to black never came. The next morning, she woke up in Frank's arms and just went on living, despite the story being over.

The Talk of Cedartown

She kept trying to recapture that same moment of perfect bliss throughout the 'honeymoon period' of their marriage, and she was successful more often than not. Frank remained the consummate gentleman, treating her exactly the way she had always wanted to be treated, relishing every moment with her and complimenting everything that she did. Both of them had their little secrets that they held back from one another, but the parts that were exposed meshed together perfectly. The only slight annoyance on Nannie's part was that Frank seemed to enjoy his whiskey a little too much and a little too frequently for her liking. She had been in the same boat back when she was married and miserable, so she didn't feel entitled to cast any aspersions on his character, but it still made her stop and wonder if he was secretly miserable, the way that she had been. The more that she pushed him to share his feelings, the more closed off he became, so she just tried to accept his words at face value and accept his heavy drinking as just a little personality quirk rather than a sign of some deeper and darker problem. After all, just because her relationship to alcohol had been defined by misery, it didn't mean that his had to be.

Prohibition was in its dying days by the time that Nannie and Frank were wed, and it was little more than a year after they'd settled in Cedartown that he was able to switch from the expensive and illegal moonshine that he had been indulging in to legally purchased whiskey that, out of habit, he continued to pour into a clay jug and hide out in the garden somewhere. But with the ready availability of liquor, Frank's drinking problem became more pronounced. He would spend his time in town after work drinking with his buddies instead of coming home to Nannie.

The beautiful home-cooked meals that she had prepared for him went cold on the table while she sat there glowering at his empty seat dancing in the candlelight. Her old dark moods had never gone far away, and when she was left in isolation it didn't take long for them to flare up. Still, she had known that Frank was a sociable man when she decided to marry him, and she would have to be a real harridan of a wife to deny him a little time with his friends. She suffered in silence, swallowed her feelings, and drifted back to her stories and the dubious social outlet of her children.

She had every reason to be happy. She had the life that she wanted, enough money that they never had to worry about making ends meet, two perfect daughters who were growing into lovely young women, and a home that could have come right out of a storybook. It was only healthy that she missed her husband when he was away. Only normal. But still this sense of doom hung overhead, and Nannie went through the motions of motherhood and housekeeping with a strange sense that all of this was just temporary, that she was just waiting for the other shoe to drop.

One of Frank's friends showed up on her porch with his hat in his hands one night after she had spent another long evening nursing her misery alone. Nannie froze in the doorway, paralyzed with the terrible knowledge that this was it, the doom she had been waiting for was finally coming to pass. But as it turned out, no terrible accident had befallen Frank beyond the one that he'd wilfully inflicted upon himself. He was in the Cedartown Police Department's drunk tank after getting into a brawl in the gutter outside the local bar, and as Nannie would discover when she went to pick him up, this wasn't the first time that he'd found himself in similar circumstances.

Back in Jacksonville, Frank had had a reputation for his drinking and a wicked temper. He had been brought up on charges twice for 'felonious assault' and even served jail time for his actions while under the influence. His family had hoped that a happy marriage and a settled life would be the perfect fresh start for him, that he was heading out of state to get a new start on life rather than running like a coward from the consequences of his actions. It would seem that they, and Nannie, had given Frank too much credit because here he was back in the same position again.

Nannie drove him home in silent fury, caught in between two powerful, but opposing, impulses. One part of her wanted to pretend that this hadn't happened, that their life together could still be the glorious dream that she wanted it to be and that Frank could go on being the perfect husband that she had always longed for but never found. The other part wanted to kill him right now for lying to her, dragging her away from everything that she had ever known. There was no middle ground or compromise for Nannie, no gradual change that she could bring about that would result in the happiness that she desired. Either everything was perfect or everything was a catastrophe, and until she could work out which it was, she was trapped in limbo.

The years rolled by with Nannie still pinned in place by indecision. She tried easing Frank off the drink, resulting in him abandoning her to go on a three-day bender with his buddies. With that failure under her belt, she tried the opposite tactic, going along with Frank when he went out drinking, matching him glass for glass until the two of them were completely smashed.

The two of them went off on one of Frank's benders, dumping the now-teenaged Melvina at a friend's house on the way out of town, but completely forgetting about Florine. The little girl came home from school to find the cabin empty and abandoned. She was there for two days before the police came out and retrieved her, scouring Polk County for Nannie and Frank before eventually turning the little girl over to her father back in Alabama. She spent an awkward weekend in the Braggs household being studiously avoided by both Charley and his new wife until Nannie came by in a blazing fury to snatch her back all over again after a few days. Nannie might not have particularly cared for her younger daughter, but she would rather die than let Charley have her.

After that misadventure, Nannie cut back on her drinking again and decided to just try to endure, to be the good wife that she had always wanted to be and to take the romantic moments as they came, even if they now came only very rarely through Frank's hungover haze. For Frank's part, he managed to hold down the same job at the factory that he had started with despite his frequent absences, but none of the advancement that he had dreamed of ever appeared. His reputation as a drunkard preceded him, and as doors were slammed shut in his face and he was denied what he felt he was entitled to, he turned more and more to the solace of the bottle.

Soured to liquor by her husband's ridiculous antics, Nannie turned to more familiar distractions for comfort. Romance fiction dominated the home, and she poured over every newspaper that came in, never writing to any of the many lonely hearts that caught her eye but always longing to. Always just on the verge of breaking away but never quite making it. Just as her dark moods had always taken her before, now they combined with a steady flow of insults from her 'gentleman' husband to convince her that she was the one at fault. The only common thread between the two 'perfect' men that she had found was her, so she began to assume that somehow she was transforming them into these bestial caricatures of the negligent husband. When Frank began to hit her in his drunken rages, her dark moods told her that she deserved it. When he did the same to her children, she just counted herself lucky that tonight she wouldn't be on the receiving end of his fists.

Despite all of this, Frank would be Nannie's husband for sixteen years in all, with both of her daughters coming to adulthood under his roof. The girls grew up into charming young women. Just as Nannie had overcome her own upbringing to seek love, so did they. Both Melvina and Florine had grown up among their mother's library of romantic fiction, but they understood the fantasy at its core, in a way that their mother had never been able to grasp. They understood that they had to marry to get out from under their father's roof, so they pursued that goal with the same determination that Nannie had, but they weren't expecting perfection or even anything particularly exciting about their husbands. All that they wanted was a better life than Frank and Nannie could provide them with.

Brief Lives

Florine's dating life slipped mostly under Nannie's radar thanks to her continuing disinterest in the girl, but Melvina was a different story. Every potential suitor was vetted by her mother to a far more exacting set of standards than she had ever used to select men of her own, as evidenced by Frank. But out of all the local men that came sniffing around when they heard rumours that the pretty young thing from the edge of the woods was ready to start courting, the only one that passed Nannie's muster was a young man named Mosie Haynes.

Mosie was eighteen years old, just like Melvina. He had a steady job in town, two supportive, but not overly-involved, parents, and a house of his own that he was more than willing to share with one of the most beautiful young women in town. Most important, from Nannie's perspective, was that he seemed to be properly respectful to both her and her daughter. A real gentleman to put right the mistake that Nannie had made with her own husband.

The two of them were wed in 1942 and settled quickly into a comfortable but quiet life, tolerating rare, brief visits from Nannie and Frank but never willingly seeking them out themselves. Nannie did her best not to take offence. She had been young once not so long ago, so she knew what those first few months of romance were like, when the whole world fell away, apart from the one you'd fallen for.

Nannie knew exactly what she'd have been doing if she had a handsome young man like Mosie at her beck and call, and it seemed that her suspicions about her daughter's activities were proven accurate when less than a year into their marriage Melvina announced that she was pregnant. Nannie expressed her happiness to the couple in extravagant terms, promised them all the help that they might need but resisted the natural urge to barge in as the overbearing mother-in-law. Part of this came from a desire to never become anything like the monstrous creature of Mother Braggs that still haunted her nightmares, but an equal part came from a feeling of profound ambivalence about the baby. On the one hand, this was the natural progression of her daughter's life—marriage and motherhood went hand in hand in the 40s—but on the other hand, it was also the end of her life.

Nannie had bitter memories of the way that children had stunted her own womanhood, robbing her of the opportunities to travel and find the great romance of her life, trapping her with a man who grew colder with each mewling mouth to feed. Nannie should have been happy for her daughter, but she could not wipe away the memory of this time in her own life—her dark moods forced her to relive them over and over. Melvina had been her opportunity to escape the same cycle, a chance for her to relive her youth without the same mistakes made again and again. But now her daughter had slipped out of reach, and there was nothing that she could do to avert the inevitable conclusion of this pregnancy. Melvina would have her baby, Mosie's eyes would begin to wander, and they would end up going their separate ways. It was inevitable. Nannie could feel that inevitability like lead lining her bones as she went through the motions of a happy grandmother.

In early 1943, the baby came so easily that Nannie wasn't even called to the hospital in time to hold her daughter's hand. Robert Lee Haynes was the apple of his mother's eye, just as Melvina had been Nannie's sole fixation. The good memories of her precious baby daughter finally broke through Nannie's deep and abiding depression. The cycle of parenthood might never end, but the cycle of misery might if Melvina had the good sense to stop right there instead of letting that fool Mosie plant baby after baby in her until she was so run-down she would rather die than go on another day.

Nannie offered up her help to her daughter without condition. She wanted nothing more than to lighten the burden that had been placed upon the girl—the burden that men would never see or understand—and the two of them connected again for the first time since Melvina was a toddler, rekindling their close relationship after years of drifting apart.

Florine, ever the afterthought, moved in with her sister to help with childcare until she had settled on a husband of her own. But it is hard to say if Nannie even noticed. The younger girl had never elicited anything more than cool indifference in her mother, so it was hardly surprising that she was ready to take the very first opportunity to get out of the house. Her relationship with Melvina had always been close, with the two

68

of them allied against the deprivations of both sets of terrible parents that they had been born to.

In 1944, as war raged across the world, a new conflict arose in Nannie when Melvina announced that she was pregnant again. It was all of her mother's worst fears realised. Another baby, and so soon after the first. That drooling beast, Mosie, hadn't even given Melvina's precious body time to heal up before he clambered back on top of her again. The baby was going to come and ruin everything. It would even ruin the fresh and tentative friendship that she had finally forged with her daughter through the common bond of motherhood. The worst part was that nobody else could see the nightmare that was about to unfold, and nobody would believe Nannie if she told them the truth about the doom that her daughter carried in her belly. Everything was going to fall apart and there was nothing that she could do to stop it.

Melvina was a small woman, and by the end of her second pregnancy, she could barely walk due to her displaced hips. When labour began for the second time in her life, in July of 1945, she genuinely believed that the pain alone might kill her. Whatever doubts still lingered in the minds of mother and daughter vanished in the heat of the moment. When the agonising contractions began, it was her mother that she cried out for, and it was her mother who answered instantly. Nannie took control of the hospital room, sending Mosie out to fetch fresh towels and glasses of cold water while she stayed by her daughter's bedside, dabbing the sweat from her head, holding her hand, and talking her through every step of the labour. Nannie even ordered the hospital staff around, and they sheepishly obeyed her barked commands. The labour stretched on through the night, but while everyone else was faltering, Nannie remained strong and resolute, getting everyone back into constant action and giving Melvina everything that she needed to push on.

Finally, after many hours, a healthy baby girl was born. Melvina was so exhausted and weakened by her ordeal and the liberal applications of ether that had gotten her through the pain, that she didn't even have the strength to hold her baby when it was all over. The baby was handed off to Nannie, who sat by her daughter's bedside with an artificial smile etched onto her face, presumably to cover her own exhaustion. By the time the doctor returned to the room, the baby was dead. Nannie quickly handed it off to the medical staff the moment that somebody noticed it wasn't breathing, but by then, it was already too late.

After the lengthy childbirth, it seemed likely that the baby had been deprived of oxygen for too long and was unable to survive for itself, but examination showed no clear cause of death. It had to be explained to Melvina over and over before she could understand, and even then she refused to believe it. Her baby couldn't be dead. It couldn't. After all that she had suffered to bring it into the world, there was no way that any loving God would snatch that baby away from her again.

Melvina returned home with Florine and Mosie the next day, still utterly distraught and hazy from exhaustion, blood loss, and the copious ether. But it was only thanks to her shattered state that she was willing to share the nightmare that she had experienced while under the influence of the ether in confidence with her sister. In that nightmare, she had seen her own mother draw a pin from her hat and push it into the soft spot on the baby's head. She had witnessed her baby being murdered by her own mother. Wasn't that a ridiculous dream? Wouldn't her sister give her some assurance that she couldn't possibly have seen what she thought that she had seen? Florine sank down onto her sister's bed in horrified silence. She had been out of the room when the baby died, passing the good news along to Mosie on the seats outside, where he lay after Nannie had chased him out. But when she returned after the baby had been declared dead, she remembered seeing Nannie quite distinctly, still sitting there by her daughter's bedside, her face in a carefully coached expression of grief as she toyed with a hatpin, making it dance between her fingers.

Just the thought of it was enough to send Melvina back into another spiral of despair. Without proof, any accusation that she made would sound like madness. It was madness. Anyone could see how devoted Nannie was to little Robert. The idea that she might have hurt one of her grandchildren was truly insane. So, both of her daughters swallowed their suspicions and tried to keep moving forward.

Mosie couldn't understand what had happened. He was a simple man, resolute in his optimism that everything was going to go his way, and the death of his baby shook his beliefs to the core. With a death that seemed so random, there wasn't even anyone that he could blame, so he gradually shifted his resentment over the tragedy onto Melvina. She made it easy for him. She was completely shattered by her baby's death and completely shut down emotionally. By the time that she had realised that they were drifting apart, it was already too late for the relationship to be salvaged, and she was too far gone to even care. More and more often, she was leaving Robert in her mother's tender loving care, trying to prove to herself again and again that there was no truth to her suspicions about Nannie and the hatpin.

With no sign of a divorce in sight, Melvina started looking for comfort in all the wrong places, actively pursuing a relationship with a soldier stationed back in Anniston, near to her father's house. She spent her weekends back in Blue Mountain, far from all of her troubles, and slept, more often than not, in her new lover's arms rather than in the uncomfortable silence of the Braggs household.

It didn't take long before Nannie caught wind of the burgeoning new relationship, and it took even less time for her to disapprove of it. She could see Melvina making all of the same mistakes that she had made, going off the rails at the very same point that her own life had been knocked off track. Everything that she had tried to avert with one brief thrust of a needle was coming to pass regardless. She cornered Melvina when she came back home after a weekend away smelling like booze, cigarettes, and cheap aftershave. She told her, in no uncertain terms, that she was ruining her life, that there was still time for her to find a new, respectable husband, that she was still young and that people were more understanding than their vitriol suggested.

Either Melvina didn't believe her mother, or she was too far gone to care. The very next Friday, she showed up with little Robert in tow, ready for another weekend-long sleepover. The women had a raging argument over the two-year-old's head. Nannie would not let Melvina leave without hearing her piece, and Melvina refused to listen to a word of it. It was her life, to live as she saw fit, and she'd had more than enough of her mother's interference. If it hadn't been for Nannie, then she would never have married Mosie to begin with. If it hadn't been for Nannie, Melvina could have stayed in Blue Mountain with her father, living together as a family instead of having to endure the insults and slaps of Frank through the years. All of the bad things that Nannie had blamed on her own parents were now dumped right onto her by the only person in the world that she cared enough about to be hurt by. It was enough to bring Nannie's cavalcade of demands and demeaning to an abrupt halt, and in the shell-shocked silence, Melvina slunk away to her car and drove away.

Nannie's rage did not leave with her daughter. It hung over her throughout the whole day as she went through the motions of caring for her grandson, and once he was settled in the little fold-out bed for the night, it descended on her once more, filling her up until she could remember nothing else. Frank was nowhere to be found, as usual, and the words on the page in front of her seemed to dance and blur, always just beyond her ability to decipher. Everything just made her angrier, and the persistent headache that had started up the moment she set eyes on Melvina did nothing to alleviate her dark mood. She lay there all night, waiting for Frank to return home so that she could take out her frustrations on him, but he never came.

With the dawn, Nannie rose red-eyed and sleepless to tend to little Robert's needs. He was breakfasted, washed, and sent out into the garden to play. Then, Nannie found herself lingering in the kitchen as she always did when she was full of this static-like energy with nowhere to put it. She started to bake, her hands going through the motions that she had learned by her own mother's elbow, without requiring any input from a brain that was too devoted to its own internal chaos to provide her body with anything resembling competent instruction. Little boys loved pastries and sweet treats, and Robert was nothing more or less than the perfectly typical little boy. She could see him dashing around the garden from her kitchen window, swinging a stick around like it was a gun and he was on the front lines in Europe, chattering away in his squeaky little voice, like gunfire had ever been so adorable. Nannie could remember Melvina at that age, before the world had taken her daughter and turned her into a harlot. How could Melvina do this to her? After all of the planning and high hopes, her life was falling apart just as surely as Nannie's had. She had always been a wilful girl, and Nannie had never been willing to beat that out of her the way that her father had taught her lessons when she was just a girl. She'd been spared the rod for too long. Melvina thought that she could do as she pleased— do whomever she pleased, too—and she was going to run into an abrupt shock if she kept it up. She was going to run right into the harsh reality of a world that Nannie had spent all her days sheltering her from. She had never known real hardship, the stomach-cramping hunger of a failed harvest or the skin-crawling memory of strangers' rough hands sliding over your bare skin. That girl needed a lesson in humility. She needed the kind of hard lesson that the world would be all too soon to give her if she didn't shape up. Something to break her out of this downward spiral that she'd set herself on.

Nannie's tempestuous mind was quick to offer up excuses and justifications for what her hands were already doing, but the truth was that she was angry. She had always been angry. The life that she wanted was perpetually out of reach. Every moment of every day was a constant struggle against her own inherent depression and the minor ordeals that she was forced to suffer through. She was furious that this was her lot in life, and while she couldn't make the people that had caused all of her troubles pay, the little boy playing out in the garden was in easy reach. He was completely innocent, probably the only person in Nannie's life who had never done her any wrong, but she could hurt him. So, she did.

There had always been a problem with rodents out here on the edge of town, just as there had been in the solid farming country where Nannie grew up, so rat poison was a constant companion throughout her life. Arsenic was the poison of choice in those days, sold in little boxes of silvery-white powder. Nannie kept hers in the kitchen on the highest shelf, to make sure nobody ever reached for it by accident. It was no accident at all when she brought it down and added it into the mixture in her bowl. The first set of cookies was ready before lunch, but she made him eat his soup before he was allowed to snack on them, like a good grandmother would. Slowly but surely, she doled out the baked treats that she had made throughout the day, gradually building up the poison inside little Robert until eventually, he was so sluggish and sore that he went to his bed early.

At any time she could have stopped, and the boy might very well have recovered. At any time she could have turned away from the course of action that her rage had set her upon. This was not a second of madness in the heat of the moment; Nannie gradually and meticulously fed poison to a toddler because his mother had failed to obey her.

That night, Nannie slept soundly with a contented smile on her face. She had finally found an outlet for all of her rage, and now she could let it go. By morning, Robert was already cold, but Nannie still went through all the frantic motions of trying to wake him, calling for a doctor and trying desperately to reach her daughter, who was off with her lover instead of staying at the Braggs house as she had promised.

The doctor examined the little boy's body, accounted for his age, and pronounced him dead of 'asphyxia,' essentially saying that the boy had expired of natural causes, in the manner that is now known as cot death. There could be no suspicion put upon Nannie at such an unfortunate turn of events. And the fact that she was so obviously racked with grief eliminated any inkling that the doctor might have had that foul play was afoot. Nannie was known to be a lovely woman, who suffered the misfortune of a bad husband as gracefully as anyone could, and she had no possible motive for killing a little boy, even if she were the kind of person who might be so inclined.

It would be the next day before Melvina came home to the news that both of her children had now died in close proximity to Nannie. All of her suspicions about hatpins came rushing back, but once again Nannie had surrounded herself with a cocoon of sympathetic locals, friends, and family so that she could not be confronted. It was a perfect repeat of her very first murder, down to the real victim that she was trying to spite coming home in shame amidst the aftermath, to face a solid wall of questions about where they had been. Melvina managed to deflect all of that in the short term by following her mother's example and launching into a wild display of grief, but in the back of her mind, some small part of her was still trying to work out if this had been a calculated move on Nannie's part or if it truly was the terrible twist of fate that she and the doctors claimed it was.

At the funeral a few days later, Melvina was back with Mosie. The grief of losing another child had her rushing right back into his comforting arms. The two of them stood alongside Florine by the graveside and watched as Nannie went into fits of hysterical sobbing before finally flinging herself into the mud in a faint. Frank had finally resurfaced from his latest binge, so it fell to him to hoist his wife back to her feet and drag her off home before she did herself an injury, but he returned to drink with his adoptive daughters once Nannie was safely squared away. He startled the girls out of their reverie with a sobering announcement. 'I reckon that I'm next.'

The three of them shared their suspicions, but there was no evidence. They couldn't even fully convince themselves that Nannie was capable of the crimes that she had committed, so how could they convince anyone else? All that they could do was watch her from a safe distance—and wait.

The War at Home

Throughout Nannie's tumultuous marriage with Frank, it may have seemed to her that the rest of the world had ground to a halt outside of her own personal bubble of depression, but sadly this was not the case. By the time of her grandson's death in 1945, the whole world was embroiled in a massive conflict that dwarfed Nannie's minor squabbles and petty cruelties in every way. The Second World War had turned every continent into a battleground, and America was no exception. In 1941, the naval base at Pearl Harbor was bombed by Japanese forces, finally drawing America into the conflict.

While there was a system of conscription in place that might have rid Nannie of her loathed husband, the sheer number of volunteer soldiers in the early days of America's involvement in the war meant that there was a genuine fear that the 'home front' of basic services and matériel production would be halted by every warm body going overseas to fight. An emergency executive order was written into law preventing anyone from the age of eighteen to thirty-seven from volunteering for military service, and before long, the randomised selection of new recruits was replaced with an administrative system to protect anyone who was involved in manufacturing from being sent off to fight.

Frank was protected by the job that he had come to resent from being sent off to die on the frontlines, but he was not protected from the contempt of the community who considered him to be a coward for not putting himself forward before the law was changed. He had lived his entire adult life as the subject of contempt and ridicule thanks to his drinking habit, but this was the first time that he felt any bite in the criticism that he received. For all of his faults, he had always considered himself to have courage, and he attributed his failure to volunteer more to his constant state of inebriation than to any desire to avoid serving his country. Every day through the four years of America's involvement in the war, he would go out drinking as normal, only to find that more of his old drinking buddies had vanished overnight, shipped off to some distant front that German U-boat attacks ensured many of them would never reach.

Every family would receive a letter when a husband or son died, but that news was very rarely conveyed along to the contemptable crowd at the local watering hole. As far as the drinking men of Cedartown knew, every time that one of their numbers went missing, they had gone to their death. Tensions were running high, with the men who were still in the lottery simultaneously excited and horrified at the prospect of their conscription, and the men who were exempted being the constant focus of their nervous energy.

Frank got into more bar-fights throughout the years of conscription than he had ever before in his life, including his wild youth, and it fell to Nannie to come and collect him off the floor every time that he got beaten. Needless to say, his own suffering soon led to his inflicting more of the same violence against Nannie to soothe his own wounded ego.

As the war abroad reached a fever pitch, so too did the indignities that Frank, and in turn Nannie, had to suffer through until finally, it all came to an abrupt and fiery end. On the sixth of August, 1945, less than a month after the funeral of Robert, the United States dropped a nuclear weapon on Hiroshima. On the eighth of August, the Soviet Union invaded Japanese territory, and America dropped a second atomic bomb on the city of Nagasaki. At the direction of the emperor, Japan surrendered unconditionally to the Allied powers, and the war came to an end, with the official announcement of surrender travelling around the world by the fifteenth August. It was a cause for celebration across America. The war was finally over, and all of the survivors were going to get to come home. Almost everyone in Cedartown treated it as a national holiday, with production in the mill grinding to a halt by midday when the frenetic pace of production that they had been pursuing all throughout the war was finally dropped.

Surprising nobody, Frank suggested that his co-workers come out for a drink with him to celebrate their great nation's victory, and for a change, they were actually inclined to go along with him. This would be a chance to clear the air before all of the boys from abroad got back home, to present a united front to the men who were going to need their support. More importantly, it was a chance for them to all feel like they were equal again, instead of half the town having to walk on eggshells while blaming the other half for their misfortune. All of Frank's old drinking buddies who had grown distant were ready to welcome him back with open arms, and the tiny silo of men just like him—who had been growing more isolated and insular as the war raged on—felt like they could breathe again. It was the happiest that Frank could ever remember being. The drinking went on and on through the day and into the night, with every single man in town coming by to buy a round, or so it seemed to the liquor-addled crowd. The camaraderie and goodwill were so bountiful that all of Frank's old sins were forgiven by the men who just a week ago would have punched the grin off his face and left him bleeding in the mud. He was on a high, the likes of which he had never experienced before. So when the bar crowd started to disperse it is hardly surprising that he tried to keep the party going. First, he went back to a friend's house, where they indulged in some of the cheap, local moonshine that had persisted long after the end of prohibition. Then, when all of the hardcore drinkers began to fall away towards dawn, he was forced to call on his wife to come and collect him.

While Nannie had always suffered these night-time trips with quiet dignity in the past, this time she found herself genuinely amused by Frank's overwhelming good cheer. It reminded her of the early days of their marriage, when the two of them still behaved like lovers instead of enemies, and she found herself laughing along with his jokes as if no time had gone by at all. For the duration of that short car ride, Nannie almost forgot all of the pointless cruelties that he had made her suffer. She almost started to think of him as a potential romantic partner again. Almost.

It is unclear whether Frank was so happy that he genuinely believed that his relationship with Nannie was salvageable or if he saw her softening attitude towards him as a sign of weakness, a chink in the impregnable armour of ice that she had formed around herself and their marital bed. But either way, he became increasingly amorous as they approached home until she was forced to pry his hand off her knee so that she could change gears. Once they were in the house, it seemed like any hint of human restraint left Frank entirely. He pushed Nannie up against a wall, smothering her with sloppy kisses and fumbling with her skirt. Up to a point, she reciprocated his advances. This was all so familiar: the smell of rye whiskey on a man's breath, the burn of his stubble on her neck, the pain where his finger dug too deeply into her thighs. It all added up to remind her of finding comfort in the arms of other men, of the teenage dalliances and desperate search for any sort of escape that had characterised her first miserable failure of a marriage. It was too much.

She took hold of his wrists and dragged his grabbing hands away before he could do more than leave some bruises. 'Get off me.'

Frank didn't seem inclined to take no for an answer. He twisted out of her grip, hooked his fingers and started tearing at her blouse. A ragged laugh escaped his lips as she writhed and struggled against him. Her resistance excited him more than her pliant submission ever had. She kicked him in the shins, but the pain barely made it through the haze of liquor. She tried to twist away from him, to deny him free access to the parts of her body that he seemed so intent on twisting until she wept, but that just gave him a better grip on her. He twisted her arm up her back until she could feel the bone creaking inside it and she cried out in pain. 'If you don't listen to me, woman, I ain't going to be here next week.'

Tears were running down her cheeks, and her teeth were gritted together to hold back a scream as he twisted and twisted. Just when she felt sure that her arm was going to snap, he stopped. He held her there at the exact moment of agony for almost a full minute until she whimpered out. 'Fine.' It was the first time that they had shared their marital bed in years, but whatever passion this place and these motions might have once kindled in her was all burnt away in the raging flames of her fury. She lay there, staring up at the ceiling, tears flooding down her face as Frank flopped around on top of her, grunting and groaning, drawing blood, sweat, and tears from his beloved wife before finally, with one great arch of his back, he was done. He passed out right on top of her, and it took all of her remaining strength to crawl her way out from underneath him and out of the bed before he could rouse himself from his drunken stupor and demand she fulfil her 'wifely duties' all over again.

She sat herself down in the quiet little library she had constructed for herself in her living room, surrounded by all of her precious tales of love and felt her own blood mixed with Frank's foul seed trickling down her leg. She would not sleep that night, just as she had not slept on the night before young Robert's death. That same rage was back, so overwhelming that it was a wonder it didn't seize full control of her body and march her through to the kitchen to draw a knife.

Frank had gotten away with a lot over the years. He had walked all over her, treated her like part of the furniture, and she had just kept her head down and accepted it because she never wanted to admit that there was something fundamentally wrong in her relationship. That was the kind of admission that might lead a person to introspection, the kind of revelation that might make a woman question why she was picking these broken monsters of men. Admitting that there was something wrong with her marriage was tantamount to admitting to some deep, dark flaw in her own psyche, and she had done absolutely everything that she could to avoid that.

Regardless of how she felt about the matter, and regardless of whatever uncomfortable justifications she was going to have to make to herself, the bottom line was that this could not stand. Her tolerance had been taken as an invitation for more cruelty, her kindness had been taken for weakness, and this last gruesome intrusion was the straw that broke the camel's back. Her husband had betrayed her trust in the worst possible way, and now he had to pay the price for that betrayal, for his destruction of her dream of a life full of love with nothing more than the petty evil of a weak-willed man of no consequence. Frank had to die. There was no other option. But while little Robert had been entirely in her power and easy to snuff out with barely a second thought, the practicalities of killing Frank were a little more complex. If he died, there would be no easy acceptance of 'cot death' or anything like that. There would be questions that needed answers, and Nannie knew that most of those questions would be directed at her. He had to die as cleanly as Robert had, with a reasonable excuse for his death already built in. She had been careless with Robert, and it had only been luck that saved her from scrutiny. She had learned her lessons from that last murder. She couldn't act on rage alone—there had to be planning and finesse when she laid her husband to rest because the whole town already knew how he abused her, and she would be the obvious lightning rod for any suspicion in the air.

Avoiding detection was only a part of the problem. Frank no longer ate any meals at home, he had always hidden his liquor so that Nannie had no opportunity to pour it away, and after he had sobered up enough to remember what he had done last night his guard was going to be up even more than usual. Poison had always been her weapon of choice—easy to use and hard to detect—but with Frank, she had no opportunity to use it at all. The distance that she had so carefully cultivated to keep herself out of his reach was now protecting him instead. She stayed well out of his way when he finally woke the following day, listening from her hiding place out in the garden as he bustled and grumbled around the house—her house—like he was entitled to every inch of it when she had earned it with a decade of hard work. Nannie was desperate to burst in and start screaming at him, but she dreaded whatever fresh horror was going to come tumbling out of his mouth next. All it would take would be a single leer and then she didn't think she would be able to control her own actions.

She stayed out in the garden all through the morning, even after Frank had staggered off to work without so much as a backwards glance. The house that she had made into a home over all of these years felt like a prison now, too claustrophobic to tolerate for even a moment. Frank had come sauntering in and ruined that for her, just like he'd ruined every other part of her life. All that she had left that was truly hers was this garden. The flowers that she had planted. The herbs that she had grown. The trees that she had picked apples from. Every part of it had been cultivated and allowed to flourish under her watchful eye. None of her plants had been allowed to grow wild and cause trouble for themselves, or cause trouble for her. None of them ever needed to be torn up from the roots because they were ruining everything else. They were perfectly under her control, and they were perfect as a result.

When she found the patch under her rose bushes that had been dug up, all of the tears that she had been holding back since last night came flooding out. Even this was ruined. Even this had been tainted by the fumbling, useless hands of some man. The one sanctuary that she had left, the one part of her that should never have been violated. And here was the evidence that it had been. She didn't even reach for her trowel—she dug into the earth with her bare hands, scooping the loamy earth away as she sobbed. What could have been so important that it was worth ruining the sanctity of her garden? What in this world was so important to Frank that he would go interfering in a place he had never shown any interest in whatsoever?

Her fingertips scraped over the hard glaze of his moonshine bottle and she froze. Her sobs turned first hysterical and then into joyous, raucous laughter. This was exactly what she needed. This was how she could get to Frank, and nobody would even blink. He'd delivered the perfect and most poetic instrument of vengeance right into her hands.

Taking care not to get mud on herself, Nannie took the bottle over to her compost heap and poured out an inch of the moonshine. She then went into the kitchen and fetched out the rat poison. She topped up the bottle until it was back to the same level, then swished it around, doing a slow and joyful waltz around her garden with the bottle in her arms and a song in her head. Once the arsenic had dissolved into the already-sharp liquor, it was the work of a few minutes to return the bottle to the ground and bury it all over again, hiding any sign that it had ever been disturbed.

As before, all of the rage that had been driving Nannie on through the long, sleepless night left her body in a rush once the act itself was complete. She was almost limp with relief. Inside the house, she barely had time to wash up and hide the evidence of her crime before she fell into a contented nap by the fireplace. She would sleep through until the evening, when she made herself a small dinner and then went to bed early, a smile still haunting her sleeping face.

In the morning, she found her husband's body outside and went to fetch the police. The corpse was practically pickled with liquor when the doctor came to examine it, so full of the local corn whiskey that the scent of it overpowered even decomposition. Frank had not been moved since the violent and painful contortions of the previous night had come to their end, so it was all too easy to construct a story from the scene. There he lay, moonshine in hand, passed out and exposed to all of the elements. Whether his heart gave out, the night's cold got to him, or cirrhosis of the liver finally finished him off, there was no suggestion that any foul play might be afoot.

There was some concern that there had been something wrong with the moonshine that had caused his sudden death—a concern that was quite pressing for the doctor, as he had been known to indulge in a little bit of illicit drinking himself—but there was nothing left in the whiskey jar for them to examine. It seemed, at a glance, that Frank had drunk it to the very last drop, although the truth was that it had been very carefully washed out in the kitchen before being returned to its incriminating position by the side of the body. No postmortem was performed, and a well-attended funeral was conducted within the week.

While both of Nannie's daughters attended the event, neither of them would go anywhere near their mother. In fact, neither one of them would ever speak to their mother again for the rest of their lives, doing their best to distance themselves from her horrific legacy. With the death of their adoptive father, they saw Nannie's actions all too clearly for the first time. Both girls finally believed that they knew what had happened to their siblings, and Melvina finally felt like she knew the cruel fate that had befallen her children. It was enough. Just enough evidence to support their suspicions. And while they may not have given a damn whether Frank lived or died, they had loved Melvina's children so intensely that even heavy suspicion was an intolerable weight on any sort of relationship with their mother.

In the aftermath of Frank's death, Nannie experienced an unexpected windfall. Early in their marriage, when things had still been going well and Frank's drinking was under control, he had taken out a fairly hefty life insurance policy on himself, to protect Nannie and his newly-acquired daughters. With his unexpected death and no hint of foul play, that policy now paid out. She had never had money before in her life, having survived on subsistence wages, and struggled every single day to stretch the limited cash that her husbands deigned to share with her into enough food to last a month. The idea of having so much money that she didn't have to worry, at a time when she had abruptly had all ties to her dependents cut, was intoxicating. If Frank had been alive, he would have drunk it all. If Charley had still been in the picture, it would have all been spent on returning some of the glitz and glamour that his mother remembered from her youth. For Nannie, the daughter of a farmer and a surprisingly canny businesswoman in her own right, there was only one investment that made sense with that sort of lump sum. She bought land. Ten acres of it on the rural outskirts of Jacksonville, Alabama. In one corner of it, she built herself a little cottage, more a library than a home. It was close enough to the town where she had grown up that she never felt homesick or lost, but far enough from all of her family and history that she no longer felt haunted by her past. Her little plot of land was readily adopted by local share-croppers and worked to its limits, providing her with a regular income to supplement the lump sum of her insurance and the tiny pensions that she had acquired over the years. For the first time in her life, she was completely financially independent, capable of taking care of her own needs without relying on a man to provide for her—along with all of the demands that the simple provision of necessities brought with it.

She was also completely alone with her thoughts for the first time. All of her desires for a better life, all of the dreams that she had harboured for a great love affair in her life, even her dreams of travelling to exotic places—suddenly they were no longer exclusively in the realm of fantasy. She could go anywhere and do anything, without anyone to tell her what to do. There was dreadful loneliness in her time out by Jacksonville. All of her family, even her beloved Melvina, had cut off ties with her in light of the rumours being spread. Her own sisters refused to believe that Nannie could ever hurt a fly, but her mother, Lou, had a better memory of the fire in the young girl whom she had raised and the lengths that she might go to spite her father if given the opportunity. She kept her distance. Nannie corresponded with her sisters by letter, due to the distance that the two of them had travelled, but she shared few details of her real life, instead preferring to regale them with tales of her plans for the future and her hopes for one more chance at love before her life was over.

Roaming Hearts

Idleness had always been the greatest sin imaginable to the Hazle family, so there was no possibility of Nannie just sitting around and wishing for a better future. She began to order newspapers from further afield, to extend the reach of her hunt for a husband into new lonely hearts columns. While her reputation locally was still surprisingly clean, albeit tarnished with associated grief, she did not feel like the dating pool for ladies her age was particularly deep.

For a fresh start and the possibility of a future untethered to her unpleasant past, she needed to cast her net wider, across state lines and around men who had previously been out of her league, as far as the socio-economic class went.

There had never been a formal class structure in the United States, but society had certainly stratified in much the same way that could be found back in old Europe. The aftermath of the war shook that system up. Suddenly, men were coming back from abroad and receiving a free higher education under the GI Bill. Home ownership was becoming available to everyone who had fought in the army, too—it was the birth of America's massive middle-class, and Nannie with her newfound position as a landowner was moving on up along with the rest of her peers, even though her journey was via a slightly more circuitous route.

Making a decision about the quality of the men that she had been approaching to date, Nannie decided that the time had come to look for an upgrade. Even though her education had been minimal, her extensive reading had given her enough of a vocabulary to pass for whichever class background she wanted to mimic. She wrote her very own lonely hearts posting and deployed it to newspapers far and wide. The response that she received was almost overwhelming. The postman began to dread the route that took him past her house because his bag was fit to burst with all of Nannie's correspondence.

Nannie selected the men she wanted to respond to very carefully, drawing out more information from each one before divulging too much herself. She had learned her lessons after her last attempt at this sort of correspondence. A man turning up on her doorstep with another marriage proposal that she felt obliged to accept due to the romance of the gesture was precisely what she was hoping to avoid. As a result, she showed a definite preference for suitors who were from further afield and who seemed contented merely with the letters, photographs, and baked goods that she was willing to dole out.

During the two years between Frank's death and her next great romance, Nannie was very rarely home. She travelled the United States by rail, visiting cities and potential suitors everywhere that she went. There are some partial records of her staying in both Idaho and New York at different times, living the high life on her new personal fortune. In the state of New York, there were some hints from conversations with friends and correspondents of Nannie that she had made a rapid arrangement to marry a man named 'Hendricks,' but no marriage licence has ever been produced to support this claim, and all official biographers of Nannie's life have been forced to set this particular husband and potential victim aside due to the lack of records, just as the police would later do during their own investigations. With the colossal population of New York at the time and the sheer volume of mysterious deaths that the beleaguered police force had to handle during those boom years, it is hardly surprising that one middle-aged man might slip through the cracks. Whether she wed or not, we do know for certain that she continued to correspond with many of the men who had taken her fancy, stringing each one of them along until she happened to be passing by their town, or possibly just vetting them more extensively than any of her previous matchmakers had bothered to do for her.

One such man was Arlie Lanning. Arlie was a resident of Lexington, North Carolina—a good two states away from Nannie's home base—and his letters were filled with the same sort of language that her romance novels had been teasing her imagination with throughout her life. Born in Alabama himself, he had settled on the East Coast after the war was over, founding a little empire for himself on that distant shore. He had never been married before, although apparently it wasn't for a lack of trying on his part. It didn't take Nannie long to translate his platitudes about 'never finding the right person to settle down with' into the most obvious truth that the man had been a horn-dog chasing after different women all of his life. He was only now realising that if he didn't settle down fast, he was going to be left alone with nobody to keep his bed warm, but even so, he didn't seem to be in any mad rush to put a ring on Nannie's finger. That wasn't enough to dissuade Nannie, of course. She had read enough tales of redemptive love to think that she had good odds of transforming a naughty boy into a good man, even if her personal experience had been the direct opposite. Besides, there was something about Arlie's quiet confidence that really worked for Nannie. He wasn't pushy about meeting her; he was barely even pushy about getting a reply. He was extremely appreciative of the pictures and treats that she sent him, without ever demanding more, and he freely offered up anything that she ever asked for in return. It seemed like another relationship made in heaven, at least on paper.

Almost two years after the end of the war and the death of Frank, Nannie boarded a cross-country train and set out on the next great adventure of her life. She was forty-two years old, once divorced, once widowed, and still as radiant and brimming over with personality as she had been as a teenager. When Arlie met her off the train in Lexington, he was bowled over by her. The pictures that she had sent did no justice to the sight of her in motion. Nannie travelled in a cloud of perfume, her makeup movie-star perfect, her clothes impeccably pressed, her curls carefully coiffed to best accentuate the long line of her neck. She knew that she was still a beauty. She did all that she could to emphasise her own attractiveness, but it was never out of conceit. Part of it was simply her obsession with glamour in all its forms, something that she was finally able to pursue actively now that her impoverished past had fallen by the wayside. Part of it was her ever-active attempts to attract the romance of a lifetime, a whole world of possible suitors that she needed to take notice of her. For the most part though, it was about comfort. Her romance stories had always been the place where she was most happy, so it was hardly surprising that she chose to garb herself in the costuming of them and did all that she could to invoke them into reality by force of will alone.

By the time that Arlie had picked his jaw up off of the railway platform, Nannie had already offered him a hand to kiss and a little package of her home cooked treats for him to enjoy after their dinner that evening. She had booked a room in the finest hotel in Lexington for the next three nights and would return home on the fourth morning. In short, this was an audition. If Arlie could impress her as much with real conversation as he had with his letters, then she would consider letting their dalliance go on. There was no doubt in either of their minds about who was in control of the situation, but the laid-back Arlie seemed to be completely fine with handing the reins to Nannie—the first man in her life who had been quite content to accept his role as a bit-part player in her grand romantic dreams.

In Lexington, Arlie was well-known; a labourer before the war who had gone on to run his own crew after his return. He'd served with distinction in the Navy during the war, earning him the respect of his peers, and while his romantic dalliances of the past would have been a source of scandal out in rural Alabama, here in the city they were barely worthy of notice. He had several family members in the area, including a sister who had fallen on hard times and sought shelter under his wing and a mother whom he had helped to relocate from

Alabama just a year back after her husband had expired. The latter fact had been a source of some alarm for Nannie initially, but beyond paying a small stipend for her upkeep, it didn't seem that Arlie doted on his mother too much. That was good—the last thing that Nannie wanted in her life was another overbearing mother-in-law trying to tell her how to live.

The single women of Lexington still considered Arlie to be something of a catch, even if none of them had quite managed to land him yet, and this strange beautiful woman from out of town was something of a fly in the ointment for many of their plans. Despite this initial frosty reception, Nannie soon won the ladies in Arlie's life over with her genuine good humour and kindness. At this moment in her life, her dark moods had been driven off entirely as she launched herself out of obscurity and misery into the person that she had always dreamed of being. As long as she stayed in the fantasy, her old life couldn't intrude—as long as she stayed focused on creating a new Nannie at the centre of a grand romance. Her depression and violent temper were completely suppressed.

Arlie was a perfect gentleman throughout Nannie's stay in town, despite the often outrageous ways that she would flirt with him, and by the end of her visit, her mind was made up about him. She had clearly been chasing the wrong kind of men all her life when by climbing just one rung up the socio-economic ladder, she could have found herself someone like him.

They made arrangements for a wedding immediately after her return home to Alabama, and within a week she was back on a train with her bags packed, ready to start her new life as Nannie Lanning. The wedding was well attended on his side, and the absence of guests on her side of the church was taken as a sign of her mysterious and exciting nature rather than as an indication that there was something wrong with her. After all, how could such a lovely and charming woman be anything but a good person?

The two of them settled into Arlie's comfortable house in town without any issue, and they were soon the very picture of domestic bliss. Nannie had a beautiful meal on the table for him every night when he came home from work. The two of them went out dancing, to the theatre, and even to the cinema on occasion, when there was a particularly romantic film on. From the outside looking in, Nannie had created another perfect marriage for herself. But the seeds of doubt and distrust had been planted in her long ago, and it would not take long before they came to fruition once more. Every moment that she was not in Arlie's company, she was riddled with suspicions about his extra-marital activities. She was not a shrill shrew of a wife, constantly making accusations, but she did establish a solid network of spies amongst the other women about town, and Arlie's movements were noted and conveyed to her daily.

The time that he spent working was actually about half of the time that he was out and about in town each day, with the vast majority of the actual physical labour that his crew undertook requiring only a little bit of guidance on his part before he moved on to bigger and better things. Instead of Frank's rotgut whiskey, the more upscale Arlie drank wines and beers, but the end result was just the same. In the beginning, he kept it under control. He was genuinely quite in love with Nannie, and he knew that his drinking and cavorting with other women was likely to upset her, as it had his many romantic partners in the past, so he did what he considered to be the only honourable thing and lied to her. What she didn't know couldn't hurt her, and as long as he kept his drinking to a reasonable level and didn't get sloppy, he could maintain both facets of his life without any trouble; the happy marriage and the free-wheeling party lifestyle.

Needless to say, it was less than a month later that he 'got sloppy.' He fell asleep at the home of one of the women that he had been having sex with, instead of returning home for his dinner as usual. Initially, this didn't seem like the end of the world—he was only two hours late for dinner. It was the first time he had slipped up in his routine, and Nannie had always been so understanding of the demands of his working life. It might have been the sort of thing that an apology, a lie, and a bunch of flowers could fix. But it wasn't. Nannie was entirely aware of where he had been and what he had been doing. He returned home to a cold and empty house. At first, he was distraught, then frantic. He searched all about town for Nannie in all of her usual haunts, fully intent on apologising and making things right, but once again, she was nowhere to be found. It was almost midnight by the time that he trudged home, some small ember of hope still burning in his heart that she had doubled-back past him, that she would be sitting in her chair by the fire or propped up on her pillows, reading, with her sly smile still plastered on her face. She was not there. But in his haste the first time, he had missed the note that she left behind on the kitchen table, beside his long-cold dinner. It read, quite simply, 'Going on a trip. Be back soon.'

It was a week before she returned. Ostensibly, she had been off checking on her house back in Alabama, ensuring that the business side of the farm was turning over properly and her investments there were safe. Yet the train she rode back into Lexington had come from up north, not the west, and the clothes, hats, and furs that she bought on her travels had all the glitz and glamour of New York lingering about them even here. Arlie didn't dare to pass comment. He was mortified by his own behaviour, horrified that he had been caught and completely contrite when it came time to admit to his faults. He apologised to Nannie unreservedly, swore off alcohol entirely, and swore that he would become the kind of husband that he had promised to be in their letters and on their wedding day.

For a little while, he even managed it. He put in more time with the work crew and brought in more money than either he or his well-off wife could ever reasonably need. His employees were delighted to see more of their boss, particularly when he got hands-on with the work again instead of just rattling off orders and heading to the bar. His sobriety came with some drawbacks however. There was no more slacking or empathy for lateness for his workers. If Arlie was holding himself to a higher standard then he intended to drag everyone else up with him, even if it meant losing his reputation as the most good-natured boss in all of Lexington. It didn't take long before his friends and family realised that he was under some sort of strain, even if they couldn't work out that he was in a deadly battle with his own addiction.

For Nannie's part, she carried on as if nothing had happened at all, presenting herself to the world as the perfect wife and homemaker, lavishing beautiful meals on Arlie every night and tending to his every need, so long as he remained loyal and truthful with her. If he had any sort of support network, then Arlie's story might have been a happy one, rather than a tragedy, but instead, he had a whole town that missed the 'old' Arlie with his good-natured jibes and casual approach to life. It didn't take much effort on the part of his workers to convince him to come out for a drink after work to celebrate a job well done. Just one drink. That was what they said to him. But that one drink was one too many, and he soon discovered that his one drink came in a great many different glasses and lasted long into the night.

He wasn't even surprised when he dragged himself home the next morning and found Nannie long gone. This time, her note was even briefer and her absence even longer. 'Back soon' apparently meant that she would return almost a month later, with the latest fashions in her new suitcases and a complete lack of explanation for her distressed husband. Arlie got back on the wagon, apologised until he was blue in the face, and cut all ties with the men who he felt had led him astray. Once again, Nannie was magnanimous and kind, while still making it perfectly clear that she was not willing to tolerate any nonsense from Arlie. He was so fixated on making things right that it never even occurred to him to question what she had been doing all this time, or who she had been doing it with.

As the years rolled on, the cycle continued. Arlie would slip up, slide into some other woman's bed or pass out in a bar and then Nannie would be off on another grand adventure across country, in the arms of another man, or another, or another. Her eternal desire to be romanced was being fulfilled by a cavalcade of new suitors who did not realise that she was married. Her need for a stable home and husband was being fulfilled by Arlie. To say that she was contented would be to grossly oversimplify the constant fluctuation of her moods and desires, but Arlie's failings gave her sufficient excuse to slink off and relieve the pressure of maintaining her façade of perfection often enough to keep things more or less in balance.

For five years, Nannie and Arlie kept their relationship alive through its ups and downs, but despite all that she did to keep the darkness at bay, it wasn't long before the little slights of a regular marriage began to mount up. All it took was the span of three months, in which Arlie actually managed to maintain his sobriety before Nannie had reached the end of her tether. From the beginning of the long winter of 1951, stretching through to the January of 1952, Arlie stayed home instead of sneaking out with his friends. No small part of this was because a lethal flu virus had hit Lexington, and hale and hearty men were dropping like flies all through the snowy season, but it was also fuelled by his genuine desire to be a better husband—a feat made easier by the removal of invitations to go out and the temptations that came along with them.

As a 'reward' for his good behaviour, Nannie spent almost a full month baking and cooking all of her husband's favourite dishes, lavishing attention on him and performing the wifely duties that she had typically preferred to fulfil outside of their marital bed during her excursions to meet up with other 'lonely hearts' across the states.

When Christmas had rolled by, once again without a single card from any of her family, something just seemed to snap. The house fell gradually into a state of poor cleanliness. The meals became leftovers, then sandwiches, then nothing much at all. Even Nannie's perpetual glamour began to crack under her husband's endless, unintentional scrutiny. She looked unkempt and bedraggled. She didn't bother to put on her makeup some mornings. Her dark moods began to seep out past the mask of kindness that she had always kept held up between her husband and reality. He had seen the real Nannie for the very first time, just a glimpse of who she really was underneath all of the lies, and she could not stand it. Abruptly, she switched back to her usual, perfectly coiffed appearance. She made a great show of setting everything right about the house, and for the first time in their relationship, offered up an apology of her own towards Arlie, even going so far as to promise to make him a special treat to make up for her poor treatment of him—a special pie. One of his favourites. Filled with sweetened, stewed prunes, with an odd, bitter aftertaste that he couldn't quite place but refused to comment on when Nannie had obviously put so much effort into baking it for him.

She called the doctor the next morning, and when he finally made it around to her house after tackling a half dozen other calls of a very similar nature, he declared Arlie Lanning dead on the spot. A passive examination resulted in the cause of death being listed as heart failure, but that was merely the shorthand that people at the time were using to refer to the flu deaths. The medical professionals did not want to spread panic. However, there was no suspicion about what had happened to Arlie, and while the whole town mourned his passing, they banded around poor Nannie in her trying time and did what they could to support the poor widow. It was the same as had happened every time that Nannie instigated a tragedy—she was the immediate recipient of all the benefits that the tragedy brought: the centre of attention, the recipient of charity and gifts. All of the kindness that she had missed out on in her early life was delivered to her in spades every time that she killed someone else. It is hardly surprising that murder soon went from being the means to the end in itself for her.

Arlie's local family took her under their wing, with his mother immediately inviting Nannie to stay with her for as long as she needed, if she wanted to be out of the house where she had lost her husband. Nannie was reluctant to leave the house that she felt she had earned through her polite play-acting over the years, but she couldn't think of a polite way to turn down the invitation and still maintain the appearance of the grieving widow. So, she packed up her mourning clothes in one suitcase and loaded the rest into boxes to be shipped back to Alabama as soon as she found the time. Her time in Lexington was coming to a close, and the sooner that she could put the town behind her, the easier it would be to outrun any stories that might get started about her.

Before Arlie's body was even in the ground, Nannie began to make quiet enquiries about collecting on his insurance policy, and about selling along the house so that she could return to her cottage in Alabama and get sunk back into the lonely hearts columns that she had been neglecting over the past half-decade—plans that were almost immediately derailed by certain arrangements that she had not been made aware of.

The Price of a Life

Arlie's will had not been updated since the wedding with Nannie, and while the majority of his limited wealth passed to her directly, certain items outlined in his old will had other destinations pre-ordained for them. In particular, there was the house where Nannie had lived for the past five years. When Arlie's sister had first moved to Lexington, she was in dire financial straits, supported almost exclusively by her brother, and while her situation was considerably more stable now, the arrangements that he had made for her to receive his house if anything happened to him were still in place. Nannie was going to be left with nothing to show for her marriage, having failed to arrange for a life insurance policy on this husband in-between her many expeditions out of town.

While she was currently living rent-free with her mother-in-law, it was an uncomfortable situation that was continuing to exacerbate the wanderlust that had driven her to kill Arlie in the first place. She felt trapped all over again, pinned in place. And without a substantial windfall to cover her new, more extravagant lifestyle, she wasn't sure how she was going to make her escape. Despite this tension, Nannie wasn't so gauche as to suggest that Arlie's house should go to her rather than his sister, although she did enjoy the extra sympathy that the same suggestion voiced by others garnered her. Poor Nannie. First she lost her husband, and now she was losing her home. Wasn't it terribly cruel?

Arlie's sister seemed strangely resistant to any sort of badgering from friends and family along those lines. She had been through hard times, and she was a survivor. She knew that letting opportunities like this pass you by were how you ended up in trouble further down the line, and without the support of Arlie, she feared that any trouble in the future could ruin her permanently. Paying no heed to the complaints didn't mean that she had no justification for ignoring them; she knew that Nannie had a house back in Alabama and an income from the farming done around it, and she wasn't shy about mentioning it if anyone complained about her 'selfishness.'

As with most things, Nannie was outwardly gracious and internally fuming about the situation, or at least she was until she came across the insurance documents for the home and realised that in case of catastrophe, the payment would come to her rather than any new owner. She had always been exceptionally good at moving quickly once a plan had formed in her mind, and while her sister-in-law was packing up all of her belongings and cancelling her tenancy agreement, Nannie was making some rapid changes of her own.

It was a long month of waiting for Nannie—trapped in the pokey, little house with her mother-in-law, as the local fire department and the insurance company investigated the fire that had gutted Arlie's house. But eventually they gave in.

Nobody could prove that the fire that had started in Nannie's beloved kitchen had been an act of arson, even if everyone suspected it and Arlie's sister wouldn't stop shouting about it. None of Nannie's belongings went up in the blaze of course—they had already been shipped back East as she graciously moved aside for her sister-in-law to take the house.

Suspicions began to swirl around Nannie as a result of the fire, and she soon realised that her mother-in-law had moved on from being her caretaker during a trying time to being her jailor, watching her every move and assessing her guilt. Nannie had all that she needed to move away, except for some way to untangle herself from the Lanning family and their expectations of her.

If she had been willing to steal away in the night without a backwards glance or any consideration of the impression that it would leave, then she had everything that she needed to do so. But the very idea that someone might think less of her, that they might suspect her of the wrongdoings that she all too frequently committed, was anathema to her and probably a significant reason why it took so long for her crimes to be discovered at all. Nannie had become an expert in managing public opinion, and she realised early on that the good opinion of Lexington hinged on the report that her mother-in-law gave about her to the local community. Luckily, she had the ideal solution already to hand. After a few days as a guest in her mother-in-law's home, Nannie insisted on helping out around the place, and while the old woman was reluctant to break up her usual routine, she had to admit that Nannie was a far better cook, so she ceded the kitchen to her.

Mrs Lanning had a long bout of illness in the early months of 1952 following her only son's death. Some thought that it was the same influenza virus that had swept through, causing such devastation. Others, such as her daughter, were convinced that it was some sort of cancer of the guts. Ultimately, the doctor took one look at the elderly woman and made his own assumptions about her general health. After idling in bed for months on end, without the strength to so much as chew any food denser than her loving carer Nannie's stewed prunes, she passed away. All of the distance that had plagued the Lanning family since the fire melted away in their grief, and Nannie and her sister-in-law were as close as real sisters again in no time at all. The whole town had seen her kindness, nursing the sickly, old woman even through her own time of grief, and the fact that the old lady's house was going to her daughter, and rendering Nannie homeless all over again, was more than enough to sway the court of public opinion back in her favour. She lingered in Lexington only long enough to see her mother-in-law buried. Then, amidst declarations of eternal sisterhood and affection, she took a train back to Alabama and her old life, several thousand dollars richer than when she'd started out.

Nannie's return to her old cottage was a bittersweet feeling. She was surrounded once more by all of her home comforts and accompanied by all of the new luxuries that she'd acquired in her travels, but she was, once again, quite painfully alone in the world. She began to pick up her usual correspondence again, getting back into the habit of writing each day before she dove back into the chaos of the lonely hearts columns all over again. But within a few weeks, she had mail back from practically her entire extended family, begging her to go and visit her sister, Dovie, who had taken ill. Notable in its absence from her correspondence was any letter from Dovie.

Usually one of Nannie's regular respondents, she was uncharacteristically silent. Nannie had barely even unpacked her things before she was loading them into a case again and heading off to southern Alabama and her bedridden sister. Dovie had been struck down by some sort of wasting sickness that, by the time that Nannie arrived, had turned her from a pretty woman in her late thirties into something resembling a skeleton draped over with loose skin. She had been trapped in her bed for two weeks with only occasional visits from family members to break up the monotony, and she was exhausted from just the effort of her shaky walks to the bathroom. Nannie immediately took control of the situation, cleaning up the house and her sister, just as she had when the girl was a baby, before settling her back into a clean bed and promising her that she would be with her through it all, to nurse her back to health, however long that took.

It seemed that Nannie's promises extended much further than her patience when it came down to it. She played nursemaid for only a week, feeding her sister by hand and caring for her every need before she came to the decision that Dovie was not going to be getting any better. There had been no marked improvement to her condition in the seven days that Nannie had been watching over her, no regrowth of muscle or change in her terrible pallor. Nannie decided that her sister was dying. Then, shortly afterwards, she decided to ease that journey along as quickly as possible, so that her death wouldn't be such an inconvenience.

She controlled everything about Dovie's life in those final days, from the times that she was helped to the bedpan through to the food and water that was provided to her. It was hardly surprising that stewed prunes were on the menu, as it was a staple of baby food and a sweet treat comparable to apple sauce for those in need of comfort, or those with bowel troubles like Dovie complained of. It was also hardly surprising when Dovie passed away after just a week of her sister's loving care. Her illness had been a topic of great discussion in the church group that she regularly attended, and from there it had spread out through the local, rural community. The funeral was small and sparsely attended, but those who were there took note of sweet Nannie's grace under pressure. Even though she had just lost a sister and a husband, to boot, she was there taking care of everyone else, serving up an impressive spread of food and doing all that she could to make life easier on Dovie's local friends. Neither of her parents were in attendance, even if her brothers made it, and it was only after Nannie had cornered those siblings and layered on the guilt that they crumbled and told her why their parents were not there: James Hazle was dead.

Nannie had very deliberately cultivated a distance between herself and her parents throughout her second and third marriages, aware of how quickly the paper-thin fiction of her life could be torn apart by someone who knew her too well. More importantly, her relationship with her parents had never recovered from her treatment at their hands as a child. With James gone, all of the rage that Nannie had felt towards him now had no outlet or direction. It had provided the baseline of fury that she felt towards all men in every relationship. But now the object of her hatred was gone, she found herself struggling to navigate without that fundamental landmark in her mental geography.

All of her plans for the future seemed to crumble in the face of this sudden change. When she was the agent of massive tectonic shifts in her life, Nannie had no trouble navigating them, but when confronted with something like this—something completely out of her control that nonetheless had a massive impact upon her—she was at a loss.

After Dovie's funeral, she fled back to her cottage in a state of distress, a state that everyone else attributed to being a witness to her sister's early demise. Nothing could have been further from the truth. She had always entertained a fantasy of getting revenge on her father for the way that he had treated her as a child. Alongside her dreams of love, it had been one of the only things to get her through the desolate loneliness of her years on the farm. Now it seemed that yet another of her cherished fantasies had been ripped away by cruel reality. She stewed at home for a few days, unable to concentrate on anything and finding all of her old distractions to be bland and unpalatable. Then, finally, when she realised that only action was going to help, she packed herself an overnight bag and headed home to the Hazle farm, for the first time since she'd fled the state to escape it.

Lou had completely transformed since the death of her husband. Like her daughter, she had finally started to flourish once she was out of his shadow. But while Nannie had escaped decades before, Lou had suffered through a lifetime of his cold indifferent cruelty before finding freedom, and she had no idea what to do with herself without the rigid structure that he had imposed on her life. She was too old now to tend to anything around the farm, and it had never managed to turn any sort of profit throughout her life, at best managing to break even year on year. To make improvements and keep things afloat, James had been in constant debt, and with his death, none of it had been forgiven. The farm would be passing into the bank's hands within a month or so. Any hope of an inheritance that Nannie or the other Hazle children might have hoped for would be vanishing with it, and Lou was facing homelessness for the second time in her life, with no possibility of supporting herself this time around. She would soon fall on the charity of her children, and they were feeling less than charitable. A lifetime in the chilling company of their father had left both of the boys emotionally stunted and interested only in the mechanics of their own survival, they had absolutely no interest in supporting an old woman to whom they felt no particular attachment—particularly when it was well-known that Nannie, her favoured daughter, had plenty of money and space to spare.

While they had fallen out of touch, Lou didn't feel any resentment towards Nannie when she showed up on her doorstep. If anything, her beautiful, glamorous daughter filled her up with pride—after all, she had not only escaped from the nightmarish life that Lou had inadvertently consigned her to, she had made something of herself, even if the thing that she had made of herself was a rich widow.

So it was, that the two widows came to live under one roof, at least for a short while so that Lou could put the last of her affairs around the destitute farm in order and prepare for the move to Nannie's cottage. Once again, Nannie felt like her life was being dragged out of her control, just as she always did when her parents were involved. What she wanted and needed meant nothing in the face of the rules passed down from on high by James, and it seemed like Lou, who had been his messenger so often, had now assumed the mantle of dictator, fully expecting to be obeyed at every turn without question. There was no threat behind any of her demands. Instead, there was something far more insidious—the pressure of expectations and public opinion. What would people think of Nannie if she abandoned her own mother? What would they think of her if she took Lou in and then treated her poorly? Societal expectations lay at her feet like an open bear trap, just waiting to spring shut on her if she failed to give in to whatever her mother wanted. And the fact that Lou seemed to be so apologetic about the whole situation just made Nannie angrier.

This was a woman who had all of the power in the world over her, someone who could have completely changed the course of Nannie's life if she had just had the courage to stand up for herself or her daughter. And now, even now, after the bogeyman of her husband was dead and buried, she was still cowed and weak. For Nannie, this was an even greater affront than any of the indignities she had quietly suffered as a child to make this woman's life easier. It called everything that Nannie knew about her mother into question. It made her wonder if instead of being another victim of James' egomania, her mother had actually been a collaborator, or even instigator, in her hellish childhood.

Nannie's world had already been thrown into chaos by the death of her father, knocked completely off balance by the loss of the pillar around which she had built her long-harboured hatred of male authority figures. But with this slow realisation that the heroic protector in her personal mythology may have been no help at all, one of the other pillars of her worldview was crumbling. Worse yet, all of her plans to get back on the horse and pursue her dreams were going to be ruined if she had an elderly mother to care for. Her entire life was slipping out of her control, so she did the only thing that she could to re-assert her mastery over her own fate, in exactly the same way that she always had.

The kindness of Nannie was the talk of Blue Mountain once more, swooping in from out of nowhere in her mother's hour of need and taking her in. She was so generous with her time, doting on the old woman as she grew sicker and sicker, preparing every meal for her mother even when the old woman ended up bedridden. The whole town turned out for the funeral when the old woman had finally passed away, and even then, as she was awash in sympathy from all sides, Nannie was the pinnacle of good grace, making sure that all of her guests were cared for and barely sparing a moment for her own grief. It was so sad—she had lost a husband, a sister, and a mother, all within just a few years. A real tragedy.

With her mother's death, Nannie became completely untethered from her personal history. Her remaining siblings had no interest in pursuing a relationship with her, her children had fled to escape their suspicions of her, and her romantic partners were all deceased, with the exception of Charley, who had brought so much scandal on himself by betraying his wife in her hour of need that nobody would ever have listened to a word he said about Nannie anyway. She felt like she was free to invent her own history, just as she invented fantasies of her future.

The Diamond Circle Club

As much as Nannie loved to deny reality at every turn, there were certain facts that no amount of tale-spinning could erase. Her dark curls were undeniably turning grey at the temples, her once svelte waist had thickened, and her elegant neckline had manifested a double-chin. When she tried to read her beloved lonely hearts columns now, she required a pair of glasses to make it look like anything more than a blur. Age and too much good food was beginning to have an effect on her attractiveness to men. The young men full of passion, who had always come chasing after her, were now in short supply, so she set her sights on a more mature sort of gentleman, moving on from her old hunting grounds in the lonely hearts columns to a more refined national organisation known as the Diamond Circle Club.

For a not inconsiderable fifteen-dollar fee, members of this club were added to a list of potential suitors, and a list of all available members, and some details about them were circulated each month to see if some romance couldn't be stimulated.

In 1953, Nannie became a member and was soon inundated with offers from across the United States. She had always known how to sell herself. Most of the men pursuing her were not interested in a quick tumble, the way that the majority of the lonely hearts respondents had been. Indeed, sex seemed to be quite low on their list of priorities so late in life. Most were looking for something closer to a maid or housekeeper—a woman to assume the role of the wives that they had lost or the mothers that they had long since outgrown. There were few genuine bachelors among their number—most men had given up on love by that age if they'd had no success before—but one of the letters that Nannie received seemed to have been from a genuine gentleman who was looking for a real romance. He was a believer in love, even if it blossomed late in life, and he was looking for a genuine companion to spend his remaining time on Earth with. He didn't have the skill with poetry that many of Nannie's previous lovers had enticed her with, but without that layer of artistry lain over his letters, they came across as almost painfully genuine, as did his compliments. Nannie didn't even suspect that there was any deception or flattery afoot when he described her as the most beautiful thing that he had ever seen, because he did not seem to be capable of that sort of thing, and because even after all of this time and a good few knocks, her ego was still a force to be reckoned with.

Charmed enough by his sweet letters and accepting that every suitor may not be the most handsome man, Nannie set out to meet Richard Morton a short while before springtime came into full bloom, taking a train northwest to Kansas. The rolling flat fields of the state held her entranced. Nannie had lived all of her life among the hilly forests of Alabama and Georgia, never truly seeing the horizon. But now, for the very first time, she could look out of the window and see the whole world rolled out in front of her like a great, open book. In all of her travels, and even in her fantasies, middle-America had never featured, but now the verdant expanse of Kansas had her enthralled, and her dreams had been furnished with a new backdrop.

Morton met her at the station, and for once it was Nannie who was in for a pleasant surprise. She had known that he was in his sixties, a retired salesman who was now looking to settle down properly in his hometown now that life on the road was behind him, but she had no idea that he was going to be tall, dark, and handsome. With a Native American father, he had inherited hawkish good features, piercing eyes, golden-tanned skin, and thick, dark hair that didn't show even a hint of grey despite his advancing years. Nannie was surprised to find herself quite smitten with him, just as she had been with Kansas. The two of them fell into easy conversation, and Nannie began to fear as the day went on that the spark she had been hoping for just wasn't there. But when it came time to retire to her hotel for the night, Richard swept her up in his arms and kissed her, leaving her to go to bed with a buzz still clinging to her skin and a tiny, brown paper-wrapped parcel containing a beautiful necklace made by a local artist.

The gifts and the toe-curling kisses continued to be lavished on Nannie throughout her stay, and before she could even write home to ask for her things to be sent along, Richard had proposed to her. Within the month, they were wed, and she had moved into his little house out on the prairie. Richard sent a letter in to the Diamond Circle Club, politely requesting that both he and Nannie be removed from their roster of available members, thanking them profusely for making the introductions that had set him on this course and calling Nannie 'the sweetest and most wonderful woman that I have ever known.'

Nannie's new home was isolated from town but idyllic, and she set to living exactly the kind of married life that she had always dreamed of having. She could look out of her window each morning and see nothing but clear, blue skies and the straight line of the horizon beyond the corn fields. She could spend her day in the kitchen or the garden as she pleased, with no children to tend to and a husband who was almost always around to keep her company. Gone were the days when she had to wonder where her husband had gone roaming. All of her fears of betrayal seemed to finally be assuaged. The days were lazy, filled only with the things that she wanted to do, and every night she settled down by the side of her contented husband to relax and watch the television—every bit the image of the American Dream come to life.

The only times that Nannie was left alone with her thoughts were on those few days when Richard had to make a run into town for supplies, and those brief bouts of total silence came as something of a relief to Nannie after the honeymoon period of a few weeks of marital bliss drew to a close. It wasn't that she didn't enjoy Richard's company, it was just that she had become rather accustomed to time alone over the course of her last few marriages. But then, the wait for him to return home started getting longer. He would hop into his truck and head into town in the morning and not return until late afternoon, some days. When she asked him what had taken so long, he would just say that he had 'dawdled.' In the early days of his dawdling, any irritation was soon washed away in the tide of gifts that he brought back to Nannie after every trip into town. She had known from his letters that he was well off, but she had no idea that he would be treating her like a princess every moment of every day, lavishing furs and jewellery on her so consistently that she barely had time to be thrilled with one gift before the next one arrived. After a month, it stopped feeling like the royal treatment and started to feel like a bombardment, as though Richard didn't know how to express affection in any way other than buying things. It hinted at a very transactional approach to romance in his history, and once the excitement of gift-giving had faded, the question of what was taking him so long in town remained.

Nannie's usual network of contacts had never had the opportunity to develop in Kansas, mainly because Richard kept her so isolated, so she had no way of really finding out what was happening when she wasn't around. Her own opportunities to head into town were few and far between, and she always had Richard on her arm when they made the trip together, so there was very little opportunity to learn more about his activities. It was only in the sacred space and brief privacy of the hair salon that she was finally able to pry some details of Richard's life from before her arrival from the local women.

As she suspected, there had been a string of younger women ahead of her, interested only in the things that Richard could buy for them in exchange for their companionship. It would have been enough to induce sympathy for the lonely, old bachelor if it weren't for the fact that some of those same younger women were still in receipt of regular gifts. One girl in particular, who was young enough to be Richard's granddaughter, had been visited by Richard every time that he was in town on one of his dawdling shopping runs, and she had been given presents that were identical in every detail to the ones that Nannie would receive later in the day. The women in the salon were surprised at how well Nannie took the news once she had instilled enough sympathy in them with her stories about her life as a woman isolated by a controlling husband, half a world away from her family. They had expected an emotional breakdown. They had expected the older woman to make a scene, but instead, it was like she swallowed the news down with a single gulp. When Richard came to collect her after her blow-dry, she met him with the same wry smile that she had parted with him on, even as the rest of the salon scowled at him from behind their magazines for tormenting that poor, sweet woman with his infidelities.

Richard had made a terrible mistake when he married Nannie with no intention of being faithful to her. His kindness, combined with fidelity, would likely have brought him a long and happy retirement with Nannie, who was so let down by the other men in her life by this point that she was willing to accept many flaws, except for this one. He may have lied about being faithful only to her, but Nannie was concealing something considerably more dangerous in her own history.

Nannie began writing to a new crop of gentlemen correspondents, making sure to note that she had been recently widowed in Kansas and was open to travel and excitement elsewhere after a lacklustre marriage. She had always been earlier to rise than her new husband, so ensuring that he never intercepted the mail was quite simple. Any letters that were addressed to her were simply slipped inside her blouse until she could find the time to lock herself in the bathroom to pour over them. The spark of romance was back in her life again, even if it was just a fantasy kindled from some crumpled-up letters, but the flames of it would soon rise up to consume the life that she had created here for herself. In amongst the many letters that she concealed about her person there were application forms for several life insurance policies on her husband. She had been caught out once when Arlie died and left everything to his sister, she wasn't planning on having to scrabble about for money again any time soon.

For all that she feared Richard reading her mail, she certainly wasn't shy about opening his while he still dozed away the morning. Bank statements, pension documents, and loan letters piled up alongside her own collected letters, and she quickly constructed a more complete picture of Richard's finances, a better picture than even he would have been capable of articulating. His house had been re-mortgaged, his pensions barely scratched the interest on his debts, and with each passing day, he was making matters worse with his extravagant spending. Even his existing life insurance policies weren't going to be enough to cover his debts when he passed away. Nannie was going to have to dip into the policies that she had taken out just to cover everything. The old fool had intended on ruining her life with his death, so selfish that he didn't care he'd be condemning her to a life of destitution after he shuffled off the mortal coil. It was clear to Nannie that she was going to have to act quickly to stop him from pushing her even further into debt with his outrageous purchases.

Three months into the marriage, Nannie made herself a widow once more. The same recipe of stewed prunes and rat poison was used, this time baked into an apple pie that she claimed was her mother's recipe. Richard went to sleep one night and simply didn't wake up the next morning. He was an old man, so there was nothing to be suspicious about as far as the doctor was concerned, and while the women of town knew about a very good motive for foul play to be afoot, none of them were even slightly inclined to share that view with the police or their husbands. If Nannie had killed her husband, as a few of them suspected, then he had it coming, and she was a local heroine.

She didn't linger for long in Kansas after Richard had died, just long enough for the bank to foreclose on his house and for the various life insurance policies that she had taken out to pay off. When all was said and done, she was up almost two thousand dollars from this marriage, paid out in the form of a half dozen separate insurance policies that she had taken out on Richard immediately after the marriage. In 1953, that amount of money was equivalent to around about twenty thousand dollars today. Not the fortune that she had hoped to make out of the arrangement, but still a substantial amount of money.

The only thing that she took the time and care to tie up before she left Kansas forever was her correspondence, sending out a letter to every man who had been writing to her in the preceding months, to inform them of her new address. She didn't want any hint of her own infidelity being left in her wake. She couldn't bear the thought of anyone anywhere knowing even one fraction of the secrets that she kept.

Wife of a Preacher

The Diamond Circle Club did not regain Nannie as a member. As excited as Richard may have been about his wonderful find amongst their number, Nannie now considered that dating pool to have been contaminated. The quality of the men that they offered—even the nicest looking and kindest men—was clearly being very poorly judged by whoever was in charge, not to mention the fact that they had allowed a murderer into their midst without a second thought. Instead, she continued her campaign of individual correspondence with the few eligible men whom she considered to be worthy of her time, making trips out to meet up with a few of them, but applying a more exacting set of standards to them beyond whether or not they could woo her. It mattered little if a man could make her heart flutter when he was doing the very same to a dozen other women. It mattered little if he was handsome if he was going to plunge her into debt or despair with his drinking and foolishness.

Nannie gradually came to realise the same thing that most older women realise when they try to date: the men who are left in the dating pool after all of the other fish have been caught tend to be the bottom feeders or the sharks. For every meeting that she arranged, Nannie came away more depressed with her lot in life. She was no longer searching for a great romance—she had let that dream die out somewhere in the last few husbands—but she was still on the lookout for a decent man with whom she might live out the rest of her days; the kind of man with solid foundations that she could build a marriage and a life on. They didn't need to set her heart aflame or fill her every moment with delights—she had come to accept that reality would never be a match for her stories and fantasies in that regard. All that she needed was a man who would not betray her trust the way that those that had come before had done. One decent man in all the world. Surely that wasn't too much to ask?

When she made her way to Oklahoma for the first time, she found it quite dull, like a poor copy of Kansas with only a hint of the greenery that she had grown up around in Alabama. Her disappointment did not extend to the man whom she had come there to meet.

Samuel Doss was a sturdily built man, but clean living meant that he didn't show all of his fifty-nine years of age on his face. Combined with a conservative haircut, his looks were more like one of Nannie's old black and white movie stars than any of the men that she had gone chasing in the last decade or more. His manner of dress was equally conservative, with tailored suits giving him the subtle appearance of wealth without any ostentatious displays. Over the course of their time together, Samuel laid out his life before Nannie's eyes with unflinching honesty. He was a state highway inspector, which took him on the road throughout the week, but on Sundays he was a lay preacher at the local church, helping to guide souls to God, as he had been delivered from the dangers of sin when he was but a young man. He never smoked, never drank, had never chased after women in any meaningful way since he was a teenager, gambling was abhorrent to him, and he considered cuss words to be a sign of poor education and breeding. He was a gentleman.

She could tell, after just a few days in his company, that none of the problems that had plagued her previous husbands were going to rear their ugly heads in this relationship, and she thought that simply eliminating all of the things that had gone wrong would be sufficient to ensure that things would go right.

In June of 1953, just a month after she had buried Richard, the wedding took place and she moved into her new home in Tulsa, Oklahoma. Samuel took the time to consider everything in his life carefully, and the swift proposal may have seemed out of character for him were it not for the long correspondence that had preceded it. All that he truly knew about Nannie after years of writing letters, on and off, was that she was a widow, an excellent cook, and a beauty even now in her twilight years. He often advised people in his flock to count their blessings, and he fully intended to follow his own advice. He may not have had any great passion for Nannie, but what did that matter when she seemed like a perfect fit for his lifestyle? He needed someone to cook and clean for him, and to provide him with comfort in his life, and she ticked all of the boxes.

Samuel had none of the bravado of Nannie's previous husbands, none of their alpha male 'king of the house' posturing either. He would help her around the kitchen if she needed it, without a second thought, and while he insisted that the house be kept clean, he was more than willing to lend his efforts to ensure that it remained tidy. He was never threatening or violent if Nannie didn't uphold his standards, only disappointed and occasionally wheedling. The problem was not that she felt threatened or bullied when she didn't uphold his standards, it was that his standards were impossibly high. His penny-pinching attitude extended to every part of his life. Nannie was not allowed to use the electric fan in the house until the temperature was 'unbearable.' When she left a room, the lights were to be switched off and the door closed to keep in the heat. If she wished to read then only the reading lamp was to be used, illuminating a single chair in the otherwise darkened chamber. Every aspect of his life was carefully regimented, with bedtime and dinnertime scheduled for each day and sex planned ahead and marked on the calendar. There was no spontaneity to any of his actions, and now there could be no spontaneity to any of Nannie's either. All of the joy that she had found in life alone was being stripped away from her until all that she was left with were the cold bones of reality to chew on. There was no room in his budget for treats or luxuries, and Nannie had to justify everything that she purchased as a necessity or suffer through the indignity of having to head back into town to return it as 'frivolous.' Gone were the choice cuts of meat that she once prepared, gone were the fancy clothes and fine wines. Studious mediocrity was Samuel's intention for her final years, all devoted to the cause of living a more holy life. Nannie couldn't abide it.

Three months into the marriage, she made a break for it, heading back to her cottage in Alabama, where she planned to lick her wounds and make plans for the next step in her life. It wasn't clear whether this was a calculated move to prompt some sort of change in Samuel, a desperate bid for freedom from the oppressive living conditions that she had been subjected to, or simply Nannie acting out. But regardless of the motivation, running away from this husband sent her on an emotional journey that she was entirely unprepared for.

On the bus ride home, Nannie felt like a weight was lifting off her shoulders. The presence of Samuel was altogether too familiar, even after all of these years, an older man with a rigid set of rules about what she should be doing with every moment of her day. A man who determined when she was allowed to experience excitement and lust and treated her like a sinful harlot for feeling anything outside of those moments. A man who treated every penny in his pocket as worth more than all of the affection that Nannie had offered up to him freely. The justifications may have changed from a desire to please her father to trying to please Our Father who art in Heaven, but the day-to-day living was identical. Samuel Doss was just another small-town bully, so set in his ways that he'd rather crush all the life out of a woman than hear any dissenting opinion. Escaping him now was like fleeing the Hazle farm all those years ago.

When she arrived at her disused cottage, a letter from Samuel was already there waiting for her. It was not the passionate outcry of a jilted lover—a man like Samuel would have found something like that far too coarse. Instead, it was a carefully reasoned explanation for why Nannie should not leave him. He had a carefully phrased non-apology explaining that he was very set in his ways after years of repetition and that she would soon fall into the same patterns alongside him as they continued their life together. After reading that section, Nannie was incensed. The man clearly understood nothing about the suffering that he had put her through. He was still just as intent on forcing her to do everything his way for the rest of their lives together.

Her father had never apologised, either. He had always been able to present some justification for why things had to be done his way, even when he was clearly in the wrong. Samuel's version of logic seemed entirely too similar to the reasoning of the man who had forced children to work the fields instead of attending school, who had treated her and her siblings as beasts of burden. She'd been a maid and cook to some of her husbands, but it had been out of a desire to please them, not this. Never this.

It took her almost an hour to calm herself enough to go back and finish reading Samuel's letter, and what she saw there just brought all of her rage back up to simmering point. He had followed up his non-apology and none too subtle insinuations about her flighty temperament with a list of some inducements to encourage her to return home to him promptly. He was trying to buy her. Doling out kindness and equality with the same reluctance that he parted with his money. The gist of the offer was quite simple: if Nannie would adopt the same habits as him and follow the regimen that he demanded, then he would place all of his money into a shared account that they could use for household purchases rather than making her come begging to him for money every time that she needed to make a purchase. If he could trust her to behave as he behaved, then he would be willing to give her equal control over the finances, just as he expected to have equal control over their home and her time.

If the wall of frost around him had broken and he had given a genuine apology for the way that he had treated her—a human apology rather than one garbed in the language of holiness— then it is quite possible that things might have turned out differently. But in that letter, Nannie once again saw the face of her father staring back at her and for the first time realised what an opportunity that this might be for her to finally get some closure. Just as James Hazle's death had thrown her into disarray all of those years ago, so now could the murder of Samuel Doss put things right again. She would finally have her opportunity for revenge. She would finally have a chance to kill the man who had ruined her. It was too tempting to pass up. All that she would need to do was wait for a suitable justification. All that Samuel had to do to sign his own death warrant was to break the compact that he was offering in this letter.

She lingered at her cottage for a day to collect some of the belongings that she'd failed to bring along when she first moved to Oklahoma and reply to some of the letters that had accumulated while she was away getting married. There were still a fair few promising suitors waiting tentatively for her reply to their last entreaty, and now that her current relationship was headed towards an early end she felt a renewed need to keep them on the hook. She invented a story about travelling, fed it to all of them, and promised to write back to them as soon as she returned home, stating with some confidence that she would be back in her Alabama cottage before three months were out.

Samuel had no idea that he had so little time left in this world. He was absolutely delighted when Nannie returned to town, and while he was far from flamboyant in his treatment of her when she arrived, there was the briefest crack in his stoic demeanour, the hint of a tear in his eye when he pulled her into his embrace. There was no break from their regularly scheduled marriage that night, despite Nannie's attempts to incite some action, but the next morning, Samuel drove her to the bank and upheld all of his promises regarding her access to his accounts. The bank manager also advised the seemingly happy couple, and Samuel changed the beneficiary of the life insurance policy that he had taken out to ensure that Nannie would be taken care of in the event that something happened to him. He didn't know it, but he had just hammered another nail into his coffin.

Nannie had never killed a husband only for the money. There had always been an emotional component to her murders. When she was entirely rational, it seemed that she could not justify them, so she had to find some point to fixate on, some reason to stoke the flames of her rage until they were sufficient to overcome whatever scruples she had about taking the life of a man who declared his love for her almost daily. If anything, the insurance payouts of her early murders had been a bonus rather than any sort of goal, but now she was falling into the same logical patterns that Samuel insisted guide every decision, and he had just provided the latest in a long line of incentives to kill him as quickly as possible.

Much of what Nannie had brought back with her from Alabama was her personal library of beloved romance books.

She displaced many of the leather-bound tomes from Samuel's shelves in the living room and replaced them with her own well-thumbed and yellowing paperbacks—stories that she had read a dozen times over that, nonetheless, still thrilled her and gave her comfort. Almost instantly, all of the magnanimous promises that Samuel had made to Nannie about relaxing his ridiculously high standards evaporated. He did not want those books in his house. When she tried to turn the conversation back on him, to point out that he spent almost every night reading, he shut her down with a snap. The books that he read were for his intellectual and spiritual betterment. They were works of literature, objects of enlightenment, and tools of education, while hers were simply trash, the lowest common denominator entertainment, designed explicitly to induce sinful thoughts and practices. To learn and improve oneself was divine, but to wallow in the filth that she had brought into his home was a guarantee of damnation in itself. She had to cast them aside if she wanted any hope of an afterlife. She had to turn away from the life of sin that had led her to being pathetic and alone in her later years, the life of sin that had rewarded her with nought but a dead husband and an ever-widening waistline. God would reward her if she turned away from that path, and Samuel would be glad to guide her to righteousness. There was no arguing with him. Samuel clearly considered himself to be the mouthpiece of God in this matter, so no matter how she argued, it would come to nothing, because the decision had already been made above Samuel's pay grade.

Nannie had never commented on the fact that Samuel didn't own a television, even though he clearly had the wealth to afford one, assuming that it was just another symptom of his thriftiness, but now she learned it was because he considered everything broadcast to be filth and degeneracy. Television rotted the brain according to Samuel, and he would have no part in the destruction of his own faculties and setting himself on course to the eternal flames of perdition. When he spoke about God, it was the only time that Nannie saw even a spark of the man that Samuel could have been. It was the only time that he raised his voice or spoke with passion, and he wasted it all on chastising her for failing to follow some nonsense rules that he had invented and tacked on to the end of the commandments.

It was safe to say that Nannie was not a religious woman. She probably would have described herself as worldly without flinching, and the idea that something as small as reading the wrong kind of book might have an impact on her immortal soul, when the wholesale slaughter of her husbands, children, grandchildren, and more had not, was laughable to her. Yet there was nothing that she could do to sway Samuel from his religious mania, and there was nothing that he could do to convince her that spiritual life had to be devoid of worldly pleasures and passions. Their worldviews were fundamentally opposed, so Nannie did what she always had when confronted with a difference of opinion with her husband: she fell silent and began laying plans to be rid of him as promptly as possible.

The Last Supper

Ultimately, she needed no greater provocation than Samuel throwing away her books. He may have dreamed of Heaven and the rest and reward that he would find there, but for Nannie, those stained paperbacks were her holy texts, and the world of imagination that they had let her escape to were her salvation from the miseries of life. Without them, she was just as distraught as he would have been if his faith had been taken away, not that he took the time to understand that.

In Samuel Doss, Nannie faced a challenge that was the direct opposite of the one she had encountered with Frank Harrelson. While Frank had never been around to eat the poisoned food that she prepared, Samuel was there every single moment that she was in the kitchen, lingering and loitering. Worse yet, he had little stomach for sweet treats, and without sugar to cover the taste of the arsenic that she had always used, Nannie was at a loss as to how to poison him. Eventually, she resorted to just stirring it into the cup of coffee that he had along with his dinner each night.

By September, this gradual build-up of poison had begun to take its toll. Samuel's appetite and strength dwindled. He shed fifteen pounds of weight and took to his bed for a week, constantly racked throughout all of this time with spasms and stomach cramps. His doctor was stumped, eventually hospitalising Samuel so that his condition could receive around-the-clock care. He was diagnosed with a massive infection of the intestinal tract and started immediately on a course of penicillin, but even with the latest medical knowledge deployed, he still did not seem to recover. He lay in the hospital, attended to by Dr Schwelbein, a gastroenterologist who specialised in cases like his, for twenty-three days before he made a recovery. His dutiful wife Nannie was there by his bedside every single one of those days, impressing everyone with her profound kindness and the deep love that she clearly harboured for Samuel.

While she was enjoying her time alone at home in-between bouts of playacting for the hospital staff, Nannie couldn't relax properly in her new home knowing that soon Samuel would be back to ruin it all over again. Each day, before she caught the bus up to see him, she would have to collect all of the books and magazines that she had been reading and carefully secret them away so that he wouldn't discover them if he happened to be released. It was ridiculous and exhausting. She found herself sticking to Samuel's prescribed bedtime just because she was so out of sorts; she didn't feel like she could enjoy anything. This was the first time that she'd made a mistake like this in her life, and she had been forced into an awkward situation by her misjudgement of the arsenic dose. Samuel was far larger and healthier than her previous husbands had been, having never lived on the borderline of poverty, and the unfamiliar delivery method meant that she couldn't be sure exactly how much was required to get the job done and how much would become noticeable without sugar to hide its distinctive flavour.

On the twenty-third day, Nannie brought her husband home. Samuel was in good spirits when he was finally released from the hospital. He was still shrunken and weak from the experience, but the pain that had been driving him to prayer every few minutes had finally abated, and he felt like life was returning to his body once more. In Nannie, he saw a new hope for the future. He had taken note of how well she cared for him through this adversity, and he believed that this could be a new start for both of them. A chance for him to loosen the reins a little, and for her to flourish as his loving wife and caretaker until death parted them. Keeping that dream alive, he was astonished to find that Nannie had prepared a beautiful spread for his first meal home—a roast of pork with all the trimmings, and a steaming hot cup of coffee, just how he liked it. She told him that the extra expense that she had gone to would not become a regular thing—she knew how much he valued thrifty living—but just this once she wanted to give him a special treat in celebration of his return home. After so long on the extremely limited diet that the doctors had insisted would aid in his recovery, and the long period before that when he had no appetite, Samuel was absolutely ravenous. Only decorum kept him from shovelling handfuls of the delicious food directly into his face. He washed down every mouthful with another swig of coffee, and Nannie, ever attentive, kept his cup topped up. After he had eaten and drunk his fill, Nannie took him through to their shared reading room to rest, settled him in his favourite seat, and placed a new, enlightening book into his hands so that he could fully enjoy the evening while she went back to the kitchen and studiously cleaned everything, taking extra care to scrub out the coffee pot. By the time that she was finished, he was already complaining of pains in his gut once more, but both he and Nannie quickly attributed it to overeating, and he began chastising himself for gluttony as she helped him hobble through to their marriage bed. He settled onto the pillows with a groan, and Nannie calmed him by pressing her lips to his forehead one last time. She returned to her seat in the other room, turned all of the lights on bright and plucked a romance magazine out from under the cushions. Then, she waited, doing her best to ignore the moans of anguish coming from the other room by vanishing into her own world of romance. A smile slowly spread across her face as she sat there in her own little pocket of light, surrounded by night on all sides. She knew that she would find love again. Love was always out there, just waiting for her. It always had been, and it always would be. All that she had to do was take one step outside her front door and it would be hers.

When the ambulance answered her call in the morning, she had done a good job of forcing herself to cry. Samuel's long bout of illness was well-known to his physician, who quickly ascribed the death to the same gastric infection that had been plaguing him. His body was sent off to the hospital morgue, and the town began to rally around the poor widowed Nannie. Everything was going according to plan, even if he had knocked her off schedule a little by refusing to die the first time around. Nannie would have sailed right through the fake grief and the funeral as always and collected her cheque before hopping a train back home to Alabama and the pile of waiting suitors sitting in her mailbox if it hadn't been for one little spanner in the works: Dr Schwelbein.

Schwelbein was a genuine expert in his field, and he had been confused about how resistant Samuel's infection had been to antibiotics during his hospital stay. When he discovered his patient's body in the morgue, just a day after Samuel had been discharged, he immediately knew that something wasn't right. Legally, Schwelbein had no right to conduct an autopsy on the body, even if he had his suspicions about the cause of death. The official report had already been filed. Still, his curiosity and overwhelming suspicions would not relent, so he did the only thing that he could to discover the truth: he approached Nannie directly and asked her for permission to conduct an autopsy on the body.

He had cornered her at home amidst a crowd of mourners and begun talking loudly about the curious death of her husband. The gathered townsfolk were fascinated to hear that, despite outward appearances, Samuel's illness had actually been terribly unusual, possibly the result of some sort of environmental contaminant that he had come into contact with as a result of his work. It could be a public health crisis if it were not investigated properly. While it may cause her some distress to know that Samuel's body was to be examined, surely she could take some comfort in the fact that doing so could save the lives of countless more. If they had been alone, it would have been possible that Nannie could talk her way out of it, but as she was, surrounded by witnesses, there was nothing that she could do but give her consent and sign the damnable doctor's permission slip. The very same appearance of respectability that had always protected Nannie also damned her now that somebody was actually investigating her crimes.

In Samuel Doss' stomach, Schwelbein found almost half of a pork roast with all of the trimmings—barely digested—the remnants of the coffee, and enough cyanide to kill a horse. It was damning evidence that could point to only one suspect.

Mere hours after the autopsy was conducted, the police arrived to take Nannie in for questioning. She denied absolutely everything, of course, but her tone was strange. She kept letting out little strangled, almost hysterical yelps of laughter, as if the idea of her killing her husband was so ridiculous that she didn't even know how to treat it seriously. By the time that they got her to the police station and into an interrogation room, she had gotten herself under control, and those bleating laughs had become a disinterested giggle. She had brought one of her magazines along from home, and she thumbed through it as the police pressed her for answers. She gave them nothing. For hours and hours, the questioning persisted without bearing fruit. The police knew that Nannie had killed Samuel, there was no doubt about it, but as long as she refused to confess to the crime, there was no guarantee of a conviction. By this point in her life, the giggling, old woman was the very image of a sweet, old grandmother, and the police had no doubt that if she were placed in front of a jury she would charm and disarm them just as easily as she kept flummoxing their interrogators.

The Giggling Granny

While the typical suspect would have had the magazine ripped out of their hands and a sturdy beating applied not long afterwards, the investigators couldn't get past the image that Nannie presented, casually deflecting any suspicion, and giggling away at the idea that she could have ever harmed Samuel. After she had spent almost a day in custody, the local police withdrew from the room no closer to a confession, which was when Special Agent Ray Page stepped in. While the local police had worked tirelessly at Nannie and left looking exhausted, she hadn't even begun to wilt under the pressure. Indeed, she seemed to be thriving thanks to all of the attention that she had been receiving. But while they were coming at her over and over again, the investigation had been rolling along out of sight, and Page had now constructed a timeline of Nannie's life. A timeline that was punctuated with mysterious deaths that benefitted her every few years.

She met Page's gaze as he walked into the room, eyes twinkling and smile still dancing over her lips. 'Oh, you are a handsome young man, but if you think I hurt anybody I'm afraid that you're as good looking as you are foolish.'

He had been observing her in-between the many phone calls that he had made that day, and he had come to believe that she was either completely insane and detached from reality or the greatest actress that he had ever seen. But either way, he was going to have to break through the wall that she had built up around herself if he wanted to get to the truth. He carefully removed the magazine from her hands and laid it down in front of him on the table, commanding her attention. 'Do you believe in ghosts, Nannie?'

The question was so out of place that it broke through her veneer of good humour and left her silent. Page pressed on. 'A few years doing my job, you start to believe in them. They don't haunt places, you see, they haunt people. I meet a lot of haunted people, doing my job. People that have done wrong and know that they have done wrong.'

Nannie giggled again. 'I keep telling you boys, I don't know what you're talking about.'

'How many husbands have you buried, Nannie? How many of their ghosts are in this room with us right now?'

The sparkle in her eyes blinked out, and for just one moment, Page could see the black abyss lurking behind her mask of sanity. She heaved a sigh but still said nothing.

'We can do this the hard way, with me running around the country gathering up the evidence of all the folks that you killed. If I have to do that, then I'll be pushing for the death penalty. But if you admit to what you've done, then things will go a little easier on you.'

There was a long moment of silence, then she let out that damnable giggle again. 'All right, all right. I put rat poison in his coffee.'

Beyond the observation window, the whole police station had just fallen deathly silent. Page had done it. He had actually done it. Nannie pressed on. 'He was a miser of a man. He wouldn't let me watch my shows on the television, he wouldn't let me run the fan even on the hottest nights. I mean... what woman could live in circumstances like that?'

Page played along. 'He sounds very cruel, Nannie.'

She let out a breath of air. Then another giggle, like she was a child who'd been caught stealing a cookie instead of a confessed murderer. 'There, you have it. Now my conscience is clear. Can I have my magazine back now?'

'If you'll tell us about your other husbands, I'll be happy to give it back to you.'

'You promise?'

Page nodded. 'I promise. Now tell me about Morton.'

Over the course of another full day, Page was able to tease out confessions from Nannie to the murder of four of her husbands. She outright denied ever doing any harm to her relatives, including her children and grandchildren, and with all of the confessions that Page already had in writing, he didn't push the old woman for total honesty. He and Nannie both knew that she had murdered every single one of the people on his list, but it wasn't like she was ever going to be getting out of prison anyway, so he felt no need to complicate the situation any further.

Nannie was arrested, and the officers fanned out across the country to begin the grisly task of exhuming her victims' bodies. Every one of them was found to be riddled with arsenic on examination. Only the bodies of her children were left undisturbed. The state had more than enough evidence to put her away and no intention of putting anyone through more trauma than was necessary. Reporters swarmed Charley Braggs, the 'one that got away,' and he earned himself a fair bit of money and fame doling out his story to all-comers.

Of course, when the police raked through Nannie's belongings back at her cottage in Alabama, they discovered that Charley was not the 'one' that got away, so much as one of many. Nannie still had a dozen suitors on the hook, ready to be reeled in the moment that she was finished with Samuel Doss. She had a selection of fresh victims just offering themselves up to her, desperate for her lethal attention.

Nannie's own fame was stoked when the reporters finally got a chance to speak to her, and her charming giggling persona stunned the whole nation. They asked her what punishment she believed that she deserved for killing Doss, and she replied, 'Whatever they choose to do to me will be on their conscience.'

A panel of psychiatrists was assembled to examine Nannie in the run-up to her trial date, but try as they might, they could not find grounds to bar her from standing trial on the basis of her mental health. She was sane, and her actions had clearly been calculated and deliberate, not acts of passion. The state only bothered to pursue a conviction for the murder of Samuel Doss, although ample evidence was available in the other cases. Nannie's trial had already turned into a circus, and they had no intention of rewarding her with more attention if they could possibly avoid it. She was due to stand trial on the second of June, 1955, in the Criminal Court of Tulsa, but her lawyers could not come up with any sort of defence for her in all of their deliberations. At their suggestion, she pled guilty on May 17th. After a brief hearing, Judge Elmer Adams sentenced her to life in prison without parole but barred the use of the electric chair due to her sex. He had no desire to deal with the personal backlash of executing a charming, old woman, who could so casually spin a tale of abusive husbands to excuse her own actions.

She was transferred to Oklahoma State Prison, where she lived out the last ten years of her life responding to mail from her many fans, both male and female. Even then, she did not give up all hope of romance in her life, kindling flirtation in many of her correspondents even if she was never likely to see the light of day again. By 1965, Nannie was transferred to the hospital wing of the prison to live out her final days in opiate-doused comfort. Leukaemia killed her in the end. Her heart was still beating as strongly as ever, but the blood that it was pumping had turned to poison. On June 2nd, at the age of fifty-nine, Nannie Doss died, completely alone.

Nannie Doss was not the typical serial killer by any stretch of the imagination. Even if her crimes had been fuelled by a desire for gratification through murder, rather than simply as a way to dispose of unwanted people in her life, the pattern of her killings was so random and unexpected that she likely would have escaped notice regardless.

Many have attributed her murderous behaviour to the head injury that she suffered in her childhood, as though it damaged some 'moral centre' in her brain, but the truth is, of course, considerably more complicated. A family historian quite readily points out that throughout the generations, both sides of Nannie's family tree had violent and angry people on display, and that Nannie's temper had always gotten her into trouble, even before the fateful bump on the head. The truth is that there were two diametrically opposed ideals driving every single one of Nannie's actions. The first was passed down to her by her father: the idea that human life is inherently worthless and that people only have value if they are producing something or can be of use to you—a common enough assertion among sociopaths. The other ideal was passed down to her indirectly from her mother: that true love was the highest of all goals.

Ironically, it was that latter ideal that proved to make her the most lethal in the long run. If she had only been instilled with a contempt for other people then she would most likely have left them well alone, but having been forced to pursue romantic relationships throughout her life, and with her happiness dependent upon the success of those relationships, the dreamy young girl was transformed into an engine of mayhem that would have kept on rolling over the lives of men forever until it was stopped, more by luck than by any sort of intervention.

The society that created Nannie, with its contempt for women as anything other than wives and mothers, also provided the perfect smokescreen for her to operate behind. Nobody could have expected that a weak and simpering woman such as her was behind a brutal series of agonising deaths by poison. The life and times that she had been born into were the perfect disguise for her actions.

To this day, the legacy of 'The Giggling Granny' lives on in public consciousness, recurring over and over in crime fiction—remembered, sometimes a little too late, each time that a wronged wife is set the menial task of preparing a meal for her husband.

About the Author

Ryan Green is a true crime author in his late thirties. He lives in Herefordshire, England with his wife, three children, and two dogs. Outside of writing and spending time with his family, Ryan enjoys walking, reading and windsurfing.

Ryan is fascinated with History, Psychology and True Crime. In 2015, he finally started researching and writing his own work and at the end of the year, he released his first book on Britain's most notorious serial killer, Harold Shipman.

He has since written several books on lesser-known subjects, and taken the unique approach of writing from the killer's perspective. He narrates some of the most chilling scenes you'll encounter in the True Crime genre.

You can sign up to Ryan's newsletter to receive a free book, updates, and the latest releases at:

WWW.RYANGREENBOOKS.COM

More Books by Ryan Green

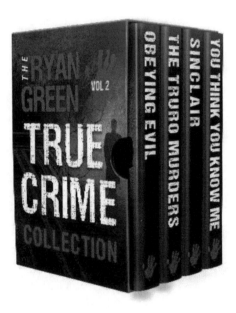

4 books for the price of 2 (save 50%)

Four chilling true crime stories in one collection, from the bestselling author Ryan Green.

Volume 2 contains some of Green's most fascinating accounts of violence, abuse, deception and murder. Within this collection, you'll receive:

- Obeying Evil
- The Truro Murders
- Sinclair
- You Think You Know Me

More Books by Ryan Green

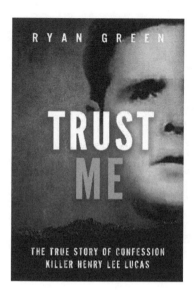

On June 5, 1983, Henry Lee Lucas was arrested for the unauthorised possession of a handgun. The police believed that he was linked to the disappearance of two females, so they used the opportunity to apply pressure and encourage a confession. After four days in custody, Lucas confessed to killing the two women.

What transpired in the following months was both peculiar and fascinating. Lucas confessed to murdering, raping and mutilating hundreds more women with his friend and lover, Ottis Toole, whilst under the influence of a satanic cult.

But there were hidden depths to the revelations. Upon further inspection, investigators found that Lucas confessed to crimes that directly contradicted others, casting doubt over what was fact and fiction.

Lucas had the answers. Could they uncover the truth?

More Books by Ryan Green

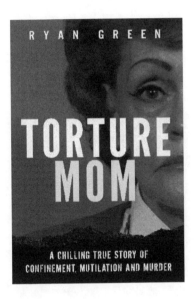

In July 1965, teenagers Sylvia and Jenny Likens were left in the temporary care of Gertrude Baniszewski, a middle-aged single mother and her seven children.

The Baniszewski household was overrun with children. There were few rules and ample freedom. Sadly, the environment created a dangerous hierarchy of social Darwinism where the strong preyed on the weak.

What transpired in the following three months was both riveting and chilling. The case shocked the entire nation and would later be described as "The single worst crime perpetuated against an individual in Indiana's history".

Free True Crime Audiobook

If you are interested in listening to a chilling True Crime story, follow the link below to download a FREE copy of *Torture Mom*.

WWW.RYANGREENBOOKS.COM/FREE-AUDIOBOOK

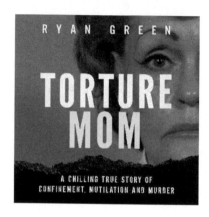

"Ryan Green has produced another excellent book and belongs at the top with true crime writers such as M. William Phelps, Gregg Olsen and Ann Rule" –**B.S. Reid**

"Wow! Chilling, shocking and totally riveting! I'm not going to sleep well after listening to this but the narration was fantastic. Crazy story but highly recommend for any true crime lover!" –**Mandy**

"Torture Mom by Ryan Green left me pretty speechless. The fact that it's a true story is just...wow" –**JStep**

"Graphic, upsetting, but superbly read and written" –**Ray C**

WWW.RYANGREENBOOKS.COM/FREE-AUDIOBOOK